365 Golden Days

Daily Empowering Messages & Writing Prompts for more self-discovery, happiness, gratitude and personal power

Sophie **Gregoire**

365 Golden Days

Daily Empowering Messages & Writing Prompts for more self-discovery, happiness, gratitude and personal power

ISBN: 979-8-9853523-2-0 (paperback)
ISBN: 979-8-9853523-3-7 (ebook)

Printed in the United States of America

Dedication

"This book is dedicated to all the souls which inspired this work and to all those who read me daily. Writers don't exist without their readers, and a writer becomes only through them. You matter more than you know."

To my mother. To powerful women, independent Empresses and builders in skirts. To all our female heroines. This is you. Such an inspiration you have always been.

To my father. To such a divinely timed entrance in my life. To the strength of a light, to the magic of a continuous guidance from the other side. This worked. I'm back to the Star.

Contents

Endorsements

"This book is a self-care gem. A writing ritual is a beautiful way to connect with your inner voice. The thoughtful prompts are in sync with the energy of the solar seasons and lunation cycles. It is an excellent choice for anyone seeking to explore and express themselves authentically."

*— **Celeste Brooks,***
Astrology by Celeste

"When I use the word "inspiration," I take a deep breath, inhale, allow Spirit to enter and animate my feelings, thoughts and imagination. So, when I say that Sophie Gregoire and her new book is INSPIRING, I meant just that. It is something to not only read, but to inhale as it works its way through your body and psyche, rearranging the cells of your days and ways one-day at a time. This book is a literal ally, sitting or walking right alongside of you, reminding you to dream and turn yourself into yourself."

*— **David Bedrick, J.D., Dipl. PW,***
Founder of the Santa Fe Institute for Shame-based Studies

"365 Golden Days is a journey to an inner-world that we can only travel through honest introspection. Sophie lights the fire for us to carry deep within ourselves, and offers us the gift of finding presence and footing in an unpredictable world. With gentle and wise guidance, 365 Golden Days is like honey poured over ripe fruit - the fruit of our becoming. The title reminds of something good that one can feel in their heart - an intuition that humanity and earth is full of kindness and love. A year of discovery; that is what is waiting for anyone reading these thoughtful pages."

— *Monika Carless*,
Author & Mystic

"I look forward to Sophie's daily intuitive messages each and every day. Her wise words support my questions and thoughts in a synchronistic way each day. To have a collaboration of these insights placed into a book, 365 Golden Days, written in a daily simplistic format, including time for reflection with writing prompts, is a dream come true!

I am forever grateful to Sophie for helping me and many others through her graceful understanding and motivational writing - the messages are unique, perceptive, inspirational and literally take my breathe away! Just what I need to hear at the exact moment! I am delighted to finally have each of these exceptional 'messages of clarity' placed together in one book. A perfect bedside table reading, a gift to all!"

— *Abby Maclean, M.A. Ed*

"Already with this first sentence of Sophie's book you can feel how she takes you gently by your hand and like a fairy, with sparkles in her eyes, encourages you to follow her on a joyful and adventurous journey to the hidden or forgotten magic treasures of your life, or - like your very best and loyal friend at your side - guides you with her questions and her pure, loving and open heart, to explore courageously your own rich soul treasures hidden deep down inside yourself.

Amazing, how much wisdom, truth, power and gentleness this young author has to offer!"

*— **Susan Dayan**,*
Chairwoman of Israeli Friends of Tibetan People

"Sophie Gregoire's 365 Golden Days holds our hand through the ebb and flow of yearly life, inspiring each day with prompts and messages that ignite the soul. Her words guide us back to our own inner knowing, pointing us straight to the heart - over and over again. Birthdays come once a year, but the gifts of 365 Golden Days deliver their magic each and every day, just when we need it most."

*— **Harmony Verna**,*
author of Daughter of Australia and
Beneath The Apple Leaves

"Sophie's book 365 golden days is a soul's journey through our daily lives. Beautifully written with powerful guidance and prompts through out. If you're seeking a gateway into your heart and mind and a journey through your spirit, then I highly recommend this book! It is a daily and continuous inspiration for all seekers. Lovely!"

— *Becky Hernandez,*
Intuitive Healer, Master Teacher & Spiritual Guide

Welcome!

Welcome to 365 Golden Days! Congratulations! By choosing this book, you are allowing yourself a magical, sparkling and fun journey of transformation!

This book was designed for you to find light at every moment and phase of the year. I will take you on a journey of personal empowerment and self-discovery over 365 days, using a few sentences or short questions each day. We will go through the several important areas of your life, whether it be love, career, meaning, identity, the past…This is your chance to explore your life on all levels and self-reflect in a deep way, yet the toolbox that this book is will be very easy to implement in your daily life, and pretty fun to follow through!

Our journey in this world is made of major stepping-stones; yet every day, every moment matters. Every step of the way, we co-create our physical reality with the Universe! Every day, we can make something count. Make a difference. Every day, we are sovereign – and we can be the awakened authors of the script of our own lives. Every day, we can give birth to a new awareness and bring something new to the light of our consciousness. This book will help you immerse yourself all year long into this sovereign, high energy, badassery.

In this book, you will find words of power and wisdom to guide you on your way. It's proven that it's the things that we do on a consistent basis that truly change ourselves. What we do or connect with daily, truly has an impact. That is why I believe that creating a daily practice only for you, every day, will do wonders. It will help you discover more about yourself and reduce your stress levels. It will help structure your daily self-care time and give it a tangible framework.

You will find in this book two distinct types of texts:

Every two days, you will find a Daily Forecast or Energy of the Day. These are empowering affirmations to support your path and guide you forward. They will help you feel and connect with the energies surrounding each of us as humans on that specific day. This also helps feeling part of a greater, grander scheme. Yes, we all are connected – and all tiny sparkles of the same vast universe! These words will have their own specific meaning for you. Let yourself flow through the words. Let them sink into your body, your belly, and your heart. Let them resonate. Let them open new pathways, new doors, within you.

The rest of the days, every two days as well, you will find writing prompts or short questions to think of and respond to! Some are there to brighten up your day, some to have you self-reflect, and some are more healing…Some start with a famous author's quotation. They are diverse, both fun and deep! They will touch the core of your soul. There is something that I'm sure of…you won't be the same lovely one at the end of this 365-day journey! In fact, it is proven that daily journaling is one of the most life-changing habits ever. It doesn't matter if you take 20 minutes or two. What matters is consistence. And you are not writing for nothing. You are writing and answering questions because this will change something in yourself, like when a gateway has been opened and afterwards can't be closed. You are writing to help you get closer to your goals, your dreams, your life vision.

Did you know that writing is a form of manifestation? Writing our goals and aspirations give them a first real, tangible form. As the saying goes, an unwritten goal is just a wish! Writing also provides with a safe and intimate space to listen to our inner selves, to be honest about our goals and dreams, our feelings and sensations. One's favorite notebook is in itself a sacred space. It's a space only for ourselves – we don't have to share it with anyone else. It is also like a secret garden. In writing, one finds the room to get closer to themselves and build a deeper form of intimacy with their soul.

How to use this book?

- I would recommend using the book every day at the same time, or approximately. In other words, choose your "best" moment: morning, evening or bedtime, or even perhaps your lunch break? What works best for you? Why not try several things before deciding? Experience is often time the best teacher!

  As for the writing prompts, ideally morning time and right before bed are the best times to journal. But don't feel restricted by this! If you feel the urge to grab your pen now, just do it! Rules are here to help create a sustainable routine, not to constrain your flow.

- Truly write what's in your heart. Don't try to make it pretty or beautiful. Don't write something to show it to somebody else, to please someone, or to be liked or approved. Write what's truly there. The truth. This is only for YOU.

- Don't worry if you miss one day, five, or even 10 days. This book is a gift from yourself to you. It is not a new constraint or a new form of forced heaviness onto your life. Of course it's great if you can make it every day and follow through, all through the year. But don't be mad at yourself if you don't.

- You have two options: buying this book at the beginning of the year, or starting it for January 1st. That seems the most obvious, but actually, everything else is fine, too. You can purchase it on June 14th and start it on June 14th, at the page referring to that day. Or purchase it on November 2nd and start on November 2nd. Anyway, it doesn't truly matter. All of these options will work exactly the same way – and all will do wonders!

- I always recommend to find or create oneself a sacred space. This may not be truly necessary to use this book and meditate on its quotations and prompts, but that could help. Also, even if becomes uncorrelated with this text, it will strengthen your spiritual practice in general.

So, what is a sacred space?

We all have a "sacred space", which is simply and basically a place, a room, a cushion, or a specific location under a tree that makes us feel good. It is a place or environment (having a bunch of crystals around your spot or carrying your favorite necklace!) that helps you create an atmosphere of safety and calmness for yourself. It is a set of circumstances that helps feeling grounded and connected to a form of higher power. Ok, so what do you personally need to create your sacred space? Is it a specific place? Objects you need to have with you? A way you like to be seated? Reflect on this and write your thoughts below!

- You will find a "conclusion" part of each month. Don't skip it! It will help you take a step back and reflect on what you've learned.

- Overall, practice being curious! Be curious about yourself! Some of your answers to the writing prompts or questions may be surprising to you! That's great! This is what we are looking for…self-discovery.

- Also, this is for you, this is a self-care tool, and this is for fun! It's ok if you don't like a few questions. It doesn't mean much about you. Just be mindful if you start letting go of ALL the questions about one specific theme, such as relationships, careers, or the past.

- And don't be too hard on yourself. If you have 15 minutes each day to devote to this, that's great. If it's three minutes, that's fine, too. It's better to go to this book often than to make it a new, heavy chore and just let it go! Also, we all have our phases. It's normal to give less time to such an exercise when one is super busy with work, kids, etc. – and way more energy when you are at the beach. Hey, we are all human!

Alright, well – let's start!

January

January 1

There is an ambitious, driven and optimistic energy that's available now. You have asked for guidance about your most important goals for the New Year, and you are starting to receive tangible clarity. You are ready to do what it takes to get there. Keep setting your intentions. Use this energy. This time is fortunate to download your vision. After that, you may be totally unstoppable.

January 2

Create your reality!

Now, let's play a little. Let's imagine you have a magic wand and everything becomes possible. If you had a magic wand, how would you spend your day today? What would you do more of? What would you do less of?

"Ester asked why people are sad. "That's simple," says the old man. "They are the prisoners of their personal history. Everyone believes that the main aim in life is to follow a plan."

— Paulo Coelho, The Zahir

January 3

Your anger felt recently burned up before slowing down into a new resolve. There are some things, types of interactions and energy leaks that you won't tolerate anymore. You are leveling up, and this means not tolerating anymore ways that are outgrown. Believe in yourself. You are powerful. Be strong and keep going on the path that you know is yours.

____

____

____

____

____

January 4

Let's go back to last year…Just for a while. If you think of the 12 previous months, what is the achievement you made or the experience you went through that you are most proud of? Don't be too shy about the magic of you. You did something golden. This, I know.

____

____

____

____

____

January 5

Your world reopens as you put yourself first. You are capable of creating change by coming back to your needs and addressing them first. The more you respect yourself, the more you attract what you deserve. You reclaim your power by feeling fuller. Big shifts are taking place as you focus on you.

January 6

Do you agree that it may be best to keep for ourselves an important vision, goal or project that we have until it's fully manifested? This may help one's golden baby-steps remain untouched by external energies or projections from others, for the time that it needs to fully hatch. What are your thoughts? Share below!

January 7

Things may still feel stagnant, but a lot is happening behind the scenes. You are on the verge of a new chapter. Don't force movement or worry. Be still. You know that you are about to receive, in perfect divine timing.

____

____

____

____

____

January 8

Now today, for a change, start with some movement. Change your first coffee taken in a hurry into a gentle walk outside, even for five small minutes. Do this even if it's raining. Notice the change for you. You are less in your thoughts now, less in the mind – more in your body, more ready for your day, and more in the present moment. Our thoughts sometimes have us trapped into overthinking or in the past. Our body is only here…now. Write down below what this experience made you feel.

____

____

____

____

January 9

There is a cleansing happening in your connections. You have made enough space within to receive higher vibrations. Don't be afraid to stand in a more powerful version of yourself.

You are moving past the image others had about you - as if reaffirming soul strength and taking a leap beyond their own projection. Some contracts are expiring, some are starting now. Trust.

January 10

When you woke up today, who was the first person you thought of and why? What do you think this means for you and for this relationship?

January 11

You may feel tense, angry, impatient, impulsive, or under pressure. These energies are turbulent yet temporary. Try and make self-care a priority. Ground yourself. See others with the eyes of love. Stay on your own sacred lane without engaging in external turmoil, and don't project inner tension externally. Focus on your well-being and allow the Universe to bless you in simple and unexpected ways. It will.

January 12

We all attract a specific type of romantic partner in our lives, at least during a phase of our personal development. Do you feel that you have a specific romantic type that's always circling back to you, even in different forms? Or maybe in the past? If that was in the past, how and why did it change? Now imagine this romantic type has something to teach you about yourself. What does this repetition, or pattern, teach you? Write a few lines down.

____

____

____

____

____

January 13

A new energy is coming at you. New beginnings are ahead. You are moving into newness. It's true, you don't know exactly yet how things will play out. But this doesn't matter. You'll move one step after the next. Magical changes are coming. You are the creator of your life. You are capable of attracting anything that your soul desires.

____

____

____

____

____

January 14

Let's speak about forgiveness. Like anyone else, you have done things you may regret. Maybe you wish you knew better. It is time to forgive yourself. Everything is an experience, a sacred lesson – there are no mistakes per se. What are you finding it hard to forgive yourself for? Self-forgiveness is a part of self-acceptance. Would you be okay with sharing this below?

____

____

____

____

January 15

A new path is progressively making itself known. It is flowing to you, and you didn't even try to make it happen that much. Destined paths tend to flow effortlessly. Certain activities, projects, or relationships are on the way out because your soul wants to embrace a new kind of alignment. Only what's supporting you in your next phase is being allowed by the Universe at this point. Trust.

____

____

____

____

January 16

Let's dream a little deeper; dream a little bigger. What are the five things you absolutely want to do in this life? These can be things you have already done and want to do again, or things you never did and utterly want to try: places to go, way of life to experience, people to meet, big projects to give birth to, truth to unveil, books to read? Write these five down.

____

____

____

____

____

January 17

A lot is moving. This year started with significant revelations or energy movements for many. The pace is fast. Let's see how everything settles down when the tide calms down a little. Be kind to yourself. Follow your intuition and gut feeling as a guiding principle. The Universe isn't leading you astray. You are safe in all times. You are safe even if the ground moves. You are levelling up and adjusting to this new moment of your life.

____

____

____

____

January 18

Good morning! I would like to know – what's your favorite music to start the day with? Maybe, share two or three. Which are the best songs for you to start the day with and help create a positive mood?

____

____

____

____

January 19

An inner voice is rising from within your soul. You can't just pretend you are not feeling the way you feel. Something needs to die there. The divine wind and the cosmic flow are pushing you in that direction. You are ready to "let go" - to stop forcing, fighting or proving yourself. To stop giving in places where you don't receive what you know is right for you. Now listen to this feeling. Acknowledge it. You don't need to run away in the exact minute though. But you know that somewhere, you've heard Truth.

____

____

____

____

January 20

This morning, I'd like you to remember of one your best mornings ever. Recall every bit of it. Write it down and include the details. Try to remember howyou felt, the colors, the weather even. Why was it so magical? What were the key words of this moment (Love, joy, harmony, peace, nature, success, fun, magic, newness, unknown, family…)?

____

____

____

____

____

____

January 21

A key part of the path is becoming much clearer to you. A weight that has been present for a long time, even years, is being lifted away. Old choices that weren't truly aligned are being put to rest, released to the ground. Your release is obvious. The Universe has heard your prayers, even those you've made in the secret of your soul. You are about to receive more and more evidence of this. You are moving forward, freer from old energy than ever before.

____

____

____

____

January 22

Talents. What are your greatest talents or traits, the ones that make you so unique and magically YOU in this world? What are the gifts, the ways, and the talents of you that make you so different from other people?

____

____

____

____

____

January 23

A lot has been seen and released in the past few days. There is more truth about your highest path. More truth about others. The feeling that you are on the verge of manifesting much more for yourself. The new is exciting and scary at once. The old just feels done. It lacks energy now. Trust yourself. One step after the next. You are the new dawn.

____

____

____

____

January 24

What's your favorite childhood memory and why? Write as much as you recall below.

____

____

____

____

____

January 25

Your reality is changing. Life is sending you an opportunity to get closer to something you longed for. You are allowing yourself to step into a new timeline. Keep moving forward even if not everybody gets where you are at right now. You will meet more of your tribe as you go. Major soul connections are on the other side of the leap.

____

____

____

____

January 26

I'm sure there are new habits you'd like to welcome in your life. Small daily changes, progressively creating major, stable impact. Share below a "great" habit you'd like to start today!

____

____

____

____

January 27

Life has brought you many revelations recently. You are powerful, yet you don't need to jump anywhere right now. Space will reveal more. Let those new pieces of yourself and of your wants sit with you. You are adjusting to a new world. There is no rush. The soul knows only divine time. Be where you are right now. You are exactly right on time.

____

____

____

____

January 28

What are the small things you do, or would like to do, to help change the world or improve the situations of others? Selfless acts, acts of contribution to the greater good, or acts of service. Acts that reach beyond your personal experience of life. Write down a few lines about your current contribution and your dreamt one. What kind of "service" person are you?

January 29

These past weeks, some new decisions, goals, and resolutions have become clear in your heart. These are important. You are about to find the strength and the stamina your soul needs to follow through. You are a new person. You are building a new reality. Keep watering your goals. See big, and then make small moves in that direction. Don't give up. The Universe is supporting you.

January 30

Yesterday, I'm sure that great or surprising things happened. Maybe someone behaved unexpectedly. Maybe you received some fantastic news. Maybe you felt confusion or pain. Maybe it was just a normal day. Whatever your situation is, what have you learned from yesterday?

January 31

You have put so much in the right direction. Surrender to the divine force now. Take this time as a sacred pause and find your breath again. You are at peace. Everything is just about to unfold as it should. The seeds you planted are growing. Relax a little as they bloom. Things will be speeding up soon.

Conclusion for January:

As we are reaching January's completion, you may find it interesting to ask yourself:

- What did you learn about yourself this month?

- Which prompt did you find the most challenging?

- Which prompt was the most enlightening to you, made you discover something about yourself or shifted the way you see things?

- Now that the month is over, and from what you've learned and written, is there a new action you'd like to take to upgrade your life for the best?

"You are not what happened.
You are the way you took to come
back.
You are the magical path – it is made
of secrets, candles, wildflowers and
strength, that you walked to recover."

Sophie Gregoire, "She is the Moon"

February

> *"Even winter, the hardest season, the most implacable,*
> *dreams, as February creeps on, of the flame that will*
> *presently melt it away. Everything tires with time and*
> *starts to seek some opposition, to save it from itself."*
> — **Clive Barker**

February 1

Today, please reflect on this quotation below. How does it make you feel, what does it make you think of? Is it changing or opening something within you?

____

____

____

____

____

"To be beautiful means to be yourself. You don't need to be accepted by others. You need to accept yourself."

– Thich Nhat Hanh

February 2

This is a powerful gateway - 2/2. The New Moon and Chinese New Year are around the corner. The energy of new beginnings abounds. It feels like you are out of a grey phase. Expect good news. Except a new-found inspiration. A flow is moving you towards a new part of your path. Big ideas, projects, or turn of events are around the corner. Feel the healing. Feel the renewal.

February 3

Let's have some fun! What are the five to 10 attributes you think are key in a soulmate for you? Don't be shy! You can still think of this even if you are already in a relationship!

February 4

A brand new page is starting. Your being has been upgraded significantly in the past weeks, and somewhere you know things have truly transformed. Some old pieces of you feel unreachable now. This all happened for the best. Doors have been closed, while others have opened. You are ready to move forward, strongly and confidently, towards this new version of you that's progressively coming out. Trust.

____

____

____

____

____

February 5

We have all experienced moments of letting go of other people. Whether that is a relationship, friends, family… one has always had a time when they had to release a bond temporarily or permanently in order to choose themselves and honor their truth. What experience of yours comes to mind now? Write below whom you had to let go of and why, and then reflect back on this decision of yours now that some time has passed.

____

____

____

____

February 6

Be strong. Life is in flux. You need rest, time to process. Not jumping in too fast or too big. Warriors slow down and contemplate to find the right way within.

____

____

____

____

February 7

What are the most frequent negative thoughts that you have experienced? Write this down! Leave this here on the paper, like one would put a suitcase down. That thought pattern is fine here on the paper. Of course, you can still take it back afterwards if you miss it! 😄

____

____

____

____

February 8

This is a space you have never been before. It took a while to get here, and it takes time to implement it all. Rest your mind, rest your thoughts. Let the seeds you recently planted grow. Allow life to meet you halfway. It will. Relax a little and watch the rewards of the energy you have given find you.

February 9

Hello, warrior of light. What was your favorite moment last week and why?

February 10

You are being asked to release control. Things are unfolding as they should with a lot going on behind the scenes. This moment is potent and charged, yet it is also a waiting room. You are waiting for more "physical events" to take place. This is planned for March. Make the most of this time of preparation. You will need it when it accelerates. Everything is sacred…organized.

____

____

____

February 11

Today, we are going to write a little more, perhaps about deeper things. Start with "I remember." Just keep going. Start with what comes. You can write many small memories and at some point, you may fall into a larger one. It doesn't matter if it is a recent memory or a very old one. Let yourself be immersed by this memory again. Go there, travel back in time. Feel it again and write about that.

____

____

____

____

____

February 12

You feel on the verge of something brand new. The incoming Full Moon in Leo will make you roar. Roar for what counts. Roar for what you believe in. Roar for what is true. Your drive and motivation to keep going in some direction is constantly reinforced. Yet, you are awaiting more support or acknowledgement from the Sky to come and greet you. Keep going, following the soul — this authentic path of your destiny. Don't make sense to everyone. Instead, be fully You.

February 13

"The love of books. My library is an archive of longings."

— Susan Sontag

Books are great companions. They help us travel, discover other ways of life, other experiences. They help us reach more of life than we could if they didn't exist. Sometimes, books can be enlightening, too. There are a few that may be life-challenging on one's journey. I remember feeling that way about The Alchemist (Paulo Coelho) for instance, or Waking the Tiger (Peter Levine). Which are your "life-altering" books that you have read? In a few words, why?

February 14

Your soul is whispering to you what's key for your next chapters now. Your desires and wants are becoming more clear, stronger. You are not the same person you were at the beginning of this cycle, six months ago. Don't quiet your wants. Don't dim your light, your uniqueness. Feel your true desires rising within you. Soon, you'll carry them forward even more.

February 15

Today, what do you feel the most grateful for?

February 16

Intense emotions and almost life-changing, deep or existentialist questions within the collective - this is happening because your long-term desires are being renewed. So much has been cleansed and shed within you. Keep believing in yourself. You have handled so many battles. You'll handle this one, too.

February 17

If you were an animal, what would you be? What inspires you about this one? What do you have in common with them? Describe things widely: their character, the places in the world they live in, their size, external aspect, fur…

February 18

New energy keeps landing in your world, seemingly pushing you out of your comfort zone repeatedly, daily. We are in a retrograde-free moment. Major turning points that will be the foundation of the rest of the year are being born, now. You feel a renewed drive within you, giving the strength, the energy and the trust in your guts you need to push through. Keep going. There are doors you never dared to take that you can move through successfully, now.

February 19

Do you know the meaning of your name? Look it up on the Internet or in books. Every name has a meaning, whether it be historical, spiritual or religious. What's the etymology of yours? Where does it come from? Which famous people have also had it?

____

____

____

____

February 20

We are approaching the end of the tunnel. The light is back as we are integrating what we have recently learned. It felt like a breakdown, yet was actually a breakthrough. Most likely, you have made a decision that involves you loving yourself even more, being in an even deeper service to You. Things have been unsettling, but in truth you were preparing for a milestone that will serve you in the long run. This is a time of great empowerment.

____

____

____

____

February 21

"Success is liking yourself, liking what you do and liking how you do it."

— Maya Angelou

Today, let's meditate on this inspiring affirmation from Maya Angelou. What comes to mind as you read it? To what extent does it apply to yourself, your life, your current job and projects? Go as deep as needed!

____

____

____

____

____

February 22

Your destiny is constantly trying to meet you more. Behind every doubt, each obstacle, each dark moment, resides a deeper layer of your healing — a higher level of your rebirth. What's happening now is what you signed up for many Moons ago. Trust. This is a karmic completion and rebirth.

____

____

____

____

February 23

Today, let's love ourselves a little more. What's your favorite body part, and why? Write down why it is so beautiful and so precious. Don't be reserved!

February 24

This is an emotional roller coaster we are in. So much is changing for good, yet you aren't fully existing in the new either. You are deciphering what's moving forward with you, what will be key for this next phase. Be gentle with yourself as you change. Find your center, your ground. March will bring more solidity to what is meant to be with you now.

February 25

Today, no matter where you live and how much you know your city and surroundings, go somewhere new. Try a new coffee shop, a new café, a new restaurant, a new local store. Perhaps a bookstore! Learn to get out of your comfort zone in places you already know, like your own city. Discovery is an energy more than a specific place. In truth, it can be anywhere! Go somewhere new.

February 26

Something is calming down after the turbulence. You have experienced a reset on several levels and are, or about to, be on the other side of it. You are about to land on the side of rebirth. The side of the new you after the storm. Walk in trust.

February 27

"Rejection is God's protection."

— Alice Hunt

Think of a time when you were rejected. How did you feel? How did you move through this phase of your life? What are the beautiful things that were born out of this phase? What did you learn about yourself at that time?

February 28

All the pieces of the puzzle are starting to come together. You are about to come out of this phase, these years of deep growth, stronger than ever before. Your next steps are about to become apparent. Let yourself be guided.

Conclusion for February:

As we are reaching February's completion, you may find it interesting to ask yourself:

- What did you learn about yourself this month?

- Which prompt did you find the most challenging?

- Which prompt was the most enlightening to you, made you discover something about yourself or shifted the way you see things?

- Now that the month is over, and from what you've learned and written, is there a new action you'd like to take to upgrade your life for the best?

"Happiness is a perfume you cannot pour on others without getting some on yourself"

Ralph Waldo Emerson

March

*"Every cold and dark phase ends and hence begins
a beautiful phase of warmth and vibrance. Don't
believe? Just notice March"*
— **Anamika Mishra**

March 1

This time has the power to make some miracles real. Come back to your vision. It can manifest in reality. You are seeing big for yourself and that's exactly how it should be. You were never too much. Magic is around you. The impossible can happen. Allow it your way.

March 2

What's the favorite picture of you that you are able to think of? Why? When was it taken, and with whom? What in the energy of that day, of that moment, is so important and precious to you?

____

____

____

____

March 3

You are reclaiming more of your gifts and power. You are allowing this rebirth freely. You are about to experience more abundance, connection and joy than ever before. Your life is reopening. You are reactivating something both old and new…your authentic self.

____

____

____

____

March 4

"I believe that through time, we progressively lose the superficial layers of skin that were not truly ourselves."

— Sophie Gregoire, "She is the Moon"

You are on a journey of self-discovery. You are progressively discovering your authentic self – or more precisely, allowing your true essence to shine outwardly…to be. This journey is a process. Through this process, you let go of what's not truly you, and in the space that's consequently created, you find the possibility to move forward in a both new and truer direction. What skin(s) of yours have you released so far? Why? How big were those letting go? What have they allowed you to become? Reflect a little, and/or write something down.

____

____

____

____

____

March 5

Physical symptoms of tiredness, even exhaustion or foggy energy… We have just moved past an interesting conjunction in the sky, making this past week intense, hard to fully understand everyone's motives and how things will unfold. More planetary bodies will be out of retrograde now. Your steps will feel clearer with less second-guessing. For now, take a big rest and let it all pass.

____

____

____

____

March 6

What would you truly like to receive in your life this month? What would you like to manifest? What is the thing that would bring so much joy to your heart and soul?

March 7

What an intense time full of recalibrations. Your body is trying to process the recent upgrades. If you feel you aren't on solid ground, you aren't alone. You are in completely unchartered territory. You need time to process. You need more information to feel things out and proceed. This being said, congratulations! This brand new phase is coming at you right now, just because you have done the work, just because you've released so much, and just because you deserve it.

March 8

The words we have said, but we'd have liked to avoid…Have you ever said something you would have liked to avoid saying? That left your mouth too soon, or with too much intensity? Are there any words you regret saying? Which are they?

March 9

This is a timeline shift that is about to permanently anchor itself after a solid, intense death and rebirth process. You were strong enough, ready enough, to receive the truth. Your life is upgrading. Follow your intuition without rush. Your energy is recalibrating. What's meant for you is almost there, and it can't pass you by.

March 10

If you are familiar with Tarot, what is the card you prefer? Why? Why does it resonate with you? Which facet of yourself do you think it describes?

March 11

Bigger forces are currently at play. The *plan*. You may try to understand things, but it's more of a Destiny time. The new astrological year is starting. You are not the same as a year ago. You need to release your fears more to flow more. You need to surrender your grip on things a little more. It's necessary to trust life. The flow of life knows what it is doing with you.

March 12

Today, please meditate on this quotation below. How does it make you feel? What are you thinking of now? Is an inner fire reawakened within? Where is the sacred spark leading you?

"The chances you take, the people you meet, the people you love, the faith that you have. That's what's going to define you."

— Denzel Washington

March 13

What a powerful time of death and rebirth we have moved through. So much intensity packed in this early stage of the year. So many emotional layers have been processed, so much energetic movement, and revelations of truth. The chaos and craziness is about to settle, helping you define your pathway to action. You are fine. Let it move through you. You will emerge from this stronger than ever before.

March 14

Today, send a text to one of your favorite people. Yes, just like that. Don't try to find a reason! Love just IS. It's made to flow.

March 15

It is big to say, but so much has happened since the beginning of the year. On December 31st, you were someone different. You have stood bravely in your truth since then and started an inner revolution for your life. Old schemes are completely gone because they were actually false. For you, they were the wrong filter. The energy is still intense but you feel committed to continue. You are reinventing yourself. Be proud.

March 16

This morning, start playfully! First thing you'll do is…dance! Wake up, no coffee, shower or stress. Turn your playlist on and let's dance! If you don't know how to dance, it doesn't matter, just move. Move by following the music rhythm. Try to be one with it, to merge with its pace. Observe how you feel. What opens within you? Are you releasing some heavy emotions? Have fun!

March 17

We are undergoing a significant reset. Our lives are being transformed and upgraded in several areas. Love, friendship, work, purpose, or even routines are evolving. Give yourself rest and congratulations for all the energies that are moving through you. You are exactly where you are meant to be.

March 18

Let me ask you, amongst your favorite people, who do you trust the most? Why?

March 19

You are releasing deep emotional material and even wounds. You are finding the bravery to self-reflect, love it all up and release what's not right for you. This is an upgrade, and to level up, you must release the baggage. You can trust the Universe fully, in all your phases, even what you seemingly did "wrong." Nothing is wrong in the eyes of the Higher Power. You can only be at this stage now because you went through it all before. Take care of yourself. This is a major time of inner work. You are aligning with what's to come.

____

____

____

____

March 20

"Be happy with what you have, while working for what you want'."

— Helen Keller

Meditate on this one today. To what extent do you agree? How much do you apply this wisdom to your own experience of life?

____

____

____

____

March 21

This is a time of major transition into the next stage of your life. You are releasing karma, old wounds and outgrown situations or patterns. You don't even have to think of it or make it happen. This is happening on its own. Give yourself some calmness, silence the mental chatter, as the Sky removes from your energetic field what is not for you anymore. Be proud of all the steps, even the lessons. Everything happened as it should to allow this rebirth. So much renewal is taking place. You are transitioning into newness.

____

____

____

____

March 22

Ancestors play a big part in our lives – as children but also later. Somewhere, we may think we are ourselves a baton – a transmitter between them and our own descendants, to the generations to come. We may feel we are a unique blend of all the energies we have in our genetics and which came before us. We have known some of our ancestors, some we have just heard about. I'm curious, who is the most important or inspiring ancestor for you at this time of your life?

____

____

____

____

March 23

The energy isn't always easy. It fluctuates and leads us back to the past, what we couldn't at that time understand, and what others or we did wrong. Underneath all this, your new creations, choices and soul contracts are stabilizing, taking form, layer after layer. You are about to release much heaviness with the Equinox. Until then, take the bird's eye view – you are constantly releasing more baggage.

____

____

____

____

March 24

We are humans. It is okay and normal to overreact at times. We overreact when we interpret something negatively too soon. We overreact when we start doubting someone's else intention. We overreact when something reminds us of a negative experience in the past, sometimes even unconsciously, and we feel triggered. A great practice is to pause when we feel triggered, before giving any response. This allows us precisely to *respond* from our higher selves, rather than *react*. In your case, when is the last time you felt you overreacted? Do you feel you could respond differently in the future, and how?

____

____

____

March 25

You are in a process of major change of your outer reality, following a phase of profound inner transformation, movement through fire and even DNA recalibrations. It's a process. Clarity will make itself known. Loud and clear. Like it did at each major step of the journey. What you want to experience now is progressively becoming more certain. Your wants. It's a new cycle. Affirm.

March 26

For every bad thing which happened today, find two good ones. The Universe always seeks balance. Please notice everything that's going *right* and is answering your prayers.

March 27

This moment could feel like you're floating somewhere. You may be feeling that you are going back and forth, that a fire has risen within, yet you meet obstacles or a sort of stillness, preventing you from fully moving forward. You are being asked to be patient as you are integrating the recent shifts and codes. You are purging the old. The more you allow this phase, the more you'll be ready to take off. Trust the pace of your path.

____

____

____

____

____

March 28

What is the ritual that you could add to your evening routine, to feel happier, more serene, and more peaceful or more grounded before bedtime? Perhaps it is making space to cuddle or communicate with your partner? Maybe it is going under the Moon and setting your intentions for the following day? Maybe it is reading a couple pages from your current book? Maybe it is turning off a few lamps and lighting up candles instead? Maybe it's making the decision to avoid all screen activity at least 30 minutes before sleep? Maybe it's listening to your evening playlist, therefore announcing to your nervous system that it's time for rest? It's scientifically proven that having a bedtime routine prepares the body and brain for sleep, as if it was given a clear signal!

March 29

Something has been cleared from your field. Changes are energetic before they are physical. A cloak of negative thinking or energy has or is about to be released from your space. Soon you will hear *truth* and receive your most expected answers. Feel the rebirth energy getting closer and closer. Appreciate this time, which isn't a void but a recalibration. You are about to find liberation from this torment, in perfect divine timing.

March 30

Doing new things from time to time allows oneself to open their mind and renew their own world. Sometimes, what was initially only "something new done out of curiosity" ends up becoming central parts of our lives! What's the new thing you tried out this month? What did you learn through it?

March 31

You are deserving of all this. Upgrading your life also means shading what no longer serves, releasing what you know is not *enough*. The last part of this purging phase is about to complete. These last emotions represent the last pieces standing between yourself and your highest manifestations. Trust the process. All is happening divinely. You are reaching the other side.

Conclusion for March:

As we are reaching March's completion, you may find it interesting to ask yourself:

- What did you learn about yourself this month?

- Which prompt did you find the most challenging?

- Which prompt was the most enlightening to you, made you discover something about yourself or shifted the way you see things?

- Now that the month is over, and from what you've learned and written, is there a new action you'd like to take to upgrade your life for the best?

"You'll learn, as you get older, that rules are made to be broken. Be bold enough to live on your terms, and never, ever apologize for it. Go against the grain, refuse to conform, take the road less travelled instead of the well-beaten path. "

Mandy Hale

April

"April hath put a spirit of youth in everything.
(Sonnet XCVIII)"

— William Shakespeare, Shakespeare's Sonnets

April 1

Warrior, you have made it. You have reached this spot of newness after the healing - a time of doubts and darkness. What's being offered to you now is powerful. Those are key opportunities for your journey. Embrace it. Move forward. Take the leap. Your energetic year is starting now. You are about to receive what will allow you to write a new chapter. Your manifestations are accelerating. Your issues are finding a resolve.

____

____

____

____

April 2

In some way, our lives are our responsibilities. In fact, we have many opportunities to choose elevated thoughts and emotions as we move through the day. What one person sees as bad, one sees as good, or as something in accordance with the divine plan. Our perspective changes our energy, and therefore what we attract to ourselves. When something wrong happens, it is also our responsibility to choose how to respond to it. For a similar situation or circumstance, dozens of distinct ways to respond actually exist. Our power precisely lies in our response.

> *"The trick is in what ones emphasizes. We either make ourselves miserable, or we make ourselves happy. The amount of work is the same."*

> — Carlos Castaneda

What do you feel about this? Do you share this perspective too?

____

____

____

____

____

April 3

You are ready to move forward big time, reaffirming your intentions. You are about to take action in the direction of your vision. It is a time of big life changes. In a light way, though. A fire is reborn within yourself. From there, you can make anything happen. Continue. You are about to clear the way, burn all that's false, manifest what's for your highest good. Auspicious energy… Feel it. Receive.

April 4

Today, try to write a letter to yourself. The self of today. The letter should be loving, soft, encouraging. Start with "dear me…" or "dear – your first name…" You want to talk to the core of you, to your heart. Bring reassurance if that's needed. Bring hope if that's what you seek. Give yourself some courage if you are moving through a rebirth phase. Alright, take a pen and start!

April 5

4/4 portal. Fresh rebirth. You are cleansing old energy that had reached completion and couldn't serve anymore in that exact same way. The *new* is entering as the *old* is leaving. Magical steps are around the corner. As if you had nothing to lose, you dare to become anew. A cloak is being removed from your energy. Light and hope are ushering in. Trust.

April 6

By manifestation, one means to connect so much with the energy of having something – of already enjoying it in our lives, or already acting "as if" – that the specific thing eventually lands in our tangible reality. It can also mean to pray with positive thoughts (as if one was sure that they would one day have it), meaning to desire something so much but without feeling any lack of energy, that one accelerates its actual landing in their own life. What matters here is to not feel the "lack" of it, but rather to already be in the energy of experiencing something, even before having it.

What is the most precious and beautiful thing you have manifested recently?

____

____

____

____

____

____

April 7

We are receiving change energy, which can be disorienting for many. Something may have pushed you to your limits. There is a sense that the old won't be back. The emotions, rather volatile or intense you may have felt these past 48 hours, are okay. You are only getting stronger, and getting to the core of what should be solved for your highest good. The discomfort is only your pathway to the light. Trust the wisdom of your journey. Soon you will be liberated from the chaos. You are getting to the other side.

____

____

____

____

____

April 8

What's your favorite color, and why? What does it mean to you? Why does it reflect your own energy?

____

____

____

____

____

April 9

The first three months of the year were full of releases and emotional shocks. Now a new dawn is available and the right actions are being shown to you. You are about to feel ready to release old cycles. Expect progresses and changes to manifest rapidly if you allow yourself to act accordingly. You have the power. You can choose what's for you and what is not for this next cycle. You are transcending a layer, restarting from a higher ground.

____

____

____

____

April 10

Life is a lot about accepting opportunities – being a Yes to what comes when it truly draws oneself. What are the opportunities around you at this stage of your life? Do they truly appeal to you? What are you unsure about? Are you still hesitating between a leap of faith or the status quo? If something truly draws you and is a full-body YES, are you capable of taking a leap, even if it's out of your comfort zone? Reflect on that.

April 11

Deep down, you know exactly what's right for you. You have been hearing the whispers within you, over and over. It is time to trust your intuition. Let the truth rise and become evident. Take some time to hear the voice within. Nothing meant to be is ever urgent. This isn't a time for rushing into things, but rather allowing what must go, to go. You are supported every step of the way. Take care of yourself and your body as you are preparing for the Eclipse reboot.

April 12

There are just things one will never be able to overlook, to truly forgive and fully leave in the past. There are things that truly, deeply, irrevocably hurt us and that cause a lasting crack in our relationships. What is "unforgivable" for you?

____

____

____

____

____

April 13

You won't be able to reach your next level if you don't take a few leaps. Change happens when you are ready. You are. The pain of leaving the old won't be as big as the joy of enjoying alignment in the physical with your highest vibration. Trust. The Universe is not leading you astray. Your most beautiful moments came from jumping out in the unknown.

____

____

____

____

April 14

Do something creative today. Write a short poem. Draw something. Dance a little. Make a bracelet. Collect flowers and make a beautiful bouquet. Bring colors to the meals you are preparing. Use your own inner beauty to create something, even small, which doesn't yet exist. It doesn't have to be perfect or even beautiful – it just has to be you!

April 15

You are in the in-between zone. Walking from one side of the bridge to the next. In this space, your clarity is formed as you are seeing what isn't acceptable anymore. On the other side, a life bigger than you expected awaits. Your craziest wishes could be fulfilled. Your most ingrained disappointments resolved. The dreams you had lost hope for could actually become true. Life is shifting. Stay on board. The discomfort is an illusion- it's doing a perfect job onto you.

April 16

What's your first memory? The oldest thing that you can recall? Write a few lines about it, try to be as specific and detailed as you can Allow emotions and sensations to resurface. Is it a good memory? Were you happy? Who is there? Is there any connection with the person that you are now?

April 17

Very auspicious energy. An issue or concern culminated to a point of no return and burned with this Full Moon, precisely in order to regain balance. A deep healing occurred. Relationships are partnerships are at the central stage now, experiencing a rebirth, a softening, a rejuvenation. You are gaining clarity about what counts now, what you want to grow in your life. You are exactly where you should be, reallocating your power and energy to what matters.

April 18

See Bigger!

If you had a magical wand, what would be your work? We are all playing a role in this life, with our entourage and in the greater scheme of things. As all of us, you have a mission. Are you here at this time to help others? To solve challenging questions? To pave the way? To be an example of abundance or of success? Connect with your heart and your belly. How are you? What's your legacy?

"All you have to do is to pay attention; lessons always arrive when you are ready, and if you can read the signs, you will learn everything you need to know in order to take the next step"

— Paulo Coelho, The Zahir

April 19

You must let go of control and your fear of losing something. This, to come back to yourself fully, and to come back to life anew. Nothing meant for you will go by you. Let go of all preconceived agendas and trust.

April 20

We all have a secret desire. Or several. Things we would love to do, even just once, at least to try them out. Maybe we don't dare sharing about these ideas with others. Maybe they are our secret garden. Nobody will know about what you are thinking of now! Here is a space of non-judgement. What is or are your secret desires? Write them down. Enjoy the feeling of self-acceptance that arises now.

____

____

____

____

____

April 21

Welcome to Taurus season! You are about to shift from a sense of volatility and craziness to a reprieve, a calmness, and some solid ground. Your sense of worthiness is reinforced. You know what your priorities are. You are about to give your energy in a devoted way to what counts. The seeds you recently planted are about to solidly grow. Out of the chaos, the truth manifests. Know that your most key buds are about to bloom.

____

____

____

____

April 22

Let's imagine your favorite date. Write how it looks like below.

- If you're in a relationship, you could suggest this to your partner and date them with excitement and curiosity. Sometimes, couples lose the initial spark between them because they don't take time anymore for the relationship truly.

- If you're not in a relationship at the moment, let's dream you're going to that magical date! It will certainly serve you, helping attract your soul mate your way.

____

____

____

____

____

April 23

The Eclipses are approaching. You can feel it. Something will have to die for the energy to be freed and for growth to happen. Watch for signs. You may already know or intuit what is about to happen. If you aren't already, you will be in Divine Time. The Universe is guiding you. Your pains, your sorrow, aren't in vain. They are your pathway to truth. They are your pathway to freedom. They are your pathway to more light.

____

____

____

____

____

April 24

Today I encourage you to try and listen, without reacting. This is what one calls "active listening". Active listening is more about receiving what the other is saying, acknowledging what they are expressing to you, asking questions to show your interest, and having them specify more of the circumstances of what they are sharing – than it is about giving unsolicited advice or offering your point of view. Often, people want to be listened to rather than given advice. If they need advice, they'll most likely ask for this in a more direct manner. Practice active listening as much as you can at work, with your friends and your family. Practice this especially if someone shares something of importance today with you. Receive their words as if you were about to write the book of that story for them. Write below what you are learning!

____

____

____

____

____

April 25

Many are moving through Tower moments. The Universe is throwing new challenges at you. Not to test you or bring you down — but to see you stand up for yourself. Reassert your power, one more time. A big transformation for your highest good is coming. Your intuition will become more and more clear. You'll have to follow through.

April 26

Today, I encourage you to reflect on the concept of happiness. What does happiness mean to you? Use the word joy if that feels best to you. What makes you happy or joyful? These words may have different meanings for each of us, because we access the energy of happiness differently. What is your own way?

April 27

This moment is powerful. As you release old patterns, you are learning to hear yourself, connecting to your needs and truth, more and more. In the midst of all the chaos, an important feeling is increasing — indicating your most heartfelt direction for the months to come. A desire or goal is strengthening itself. You are about to see that most of your fears about getting there are irrelevant.

____

____

____

____

____

April 28

> *"Be fearless in the pursuit of what makes your soul on fire."*
>
> – Jennifer Lee

We all have an inner calling, something that we know we must do. Or at least try. Maybe it's not something that we were expecting ourselves to like, or others were expecting us to resonate with either. Maybe, what truly sets our soul on fire somehow disturbs the status quo, the roles we are supposed to occupy or even the plans we had for our own lives. But that's the thing with soul callings. They always end up winning, because the power of *truth* is stronger than any other. What's truly aligned with our hearts always ends up resurfacing. So, it's best to acknowledge the fire within and follow it, step by step. Today, let's give this commitment to yourself. Let's not silence anymore the true callings of your inner self. Any thoughts?

____

____

____

____

April 29

A new energy, perhaps that you never experienced so far, is now fully present. As you find stillness within yourself and the recent storms, you are unearthing new answers about what you want for your life. What you deserve is gaining power - helping you shed old ground. The more you say *no* to what's not aligned, the closer you get to your blessings and desired manifestations. You are experiencing an active cleansing, cleaning your own path. Daring to express true *yes* and true *no* based on what's truly aligned. Keep going. Your key changes require your utmost bravery.

____

____

____

____

April 30

Let's end this month in beauty, and with a key question. A profound one even. Name and describe five key events or moments that have shaped your life and the person that you are now. Those are the pillars of your current identity.

____

____

____

____

____

Conclusion for April:

As we are reaching April's completion, you may find it interesting to ask yourself:

- What did you learn about yourself this month?

- Which prompt did you find the most challenging?

- Which prompt was the most enlightening to you, made you discover something about yourself or shifted the way you see things?

- Now that the month is over, and from what you've learned and written, is there a new action you'd like to take to upgrade your life for the best?

"Just because you are happy doesn't mean the day is perfect. It means that you have looked beyond its imperfections."

Bob Marley

May

"Then you have to remember to be thankful; but in May one simply can't help being thankful . . . that they are alive, if for nothing else. I feel exactly as Eve must have felt in the garden of Eden before the trouble began."

— L.M. Montgomery, Anne of Avonlea

May 1

A new time is starting for you. Abundance at all levels is about to manifest. You have been through a moment of doubts, life lessons, or void recently. So much cleansing has happened. You are gently coming out of this, allowing your energy to move forward in the direction that's truly calling you. Accept the movement. Accept to release what is holding you back so that you can embrace more of your destiny. Trust. You are going somewhere beautiful.

____

____

____

____

May 2

Today, let's try to smile as much as you can. It's proven that smiling does change one's mood, uplifts them. If you practice smiling more, you'll receive more smiles. If you practice smiling more today, I'm pretty sure you'll feel better. Experience this. Was that true for you?

____

____

____

____

May 3

Energy of major change is around each of us. You are finding your power again, opening to a portal of massive positive transformation. Dreams can come true. You are able to retrieve major parts of yourself, that you may have lost or were disconnected from for so long. The more you love yourself, the more you find the strength to release what's not aligned. You are manifesting big time. You are hearing the calling. Follow the path of your soul.

May 4

Today, let's reflect a little more on your past. Who are the five people that had the most profound, significant, impact on your life? Write their names below, and describe with a of couple sentences for each of them why their impact was big for you.

May 5

A phase of healing and depth is about to end. You had to do this shadow work and face these parts of yourself. But now a new, lighter energy is landing. Let it implement. Infuse your body, your heart, your cells. The cleansing is now complete. You are being moved step by step in the right direction.

May 6

Today, no matter what happens, repeat to yourself, as often as possible "I AM WORTHY." Through the ups and downs. The good moments and the others. The good news I hope, or whatever comes at you. Make it your anthem for today. Say it out loud or in your mind as much as you can. All the time maybe. Hey you, you are worthy!

May 7

You are starting to feel out what your future looks like. Premonitions. Soul callings. This time is powerful. Full of energy, guides and ancestors, leading you. If you can find space and listen, you'll hear. If you can stop the mind chatter about what should be, should have been, or used to be true - you'll be able to find your inner strength, the draw towards your unique golden path, inviting you. Have faith. All of this is divine.

May 8

"It is up to us, whether to be happy for what we have, or to be unhappy for what we don't have."

— Shon Mehta

Sometimes, we don't realize how precious what we already have is. We are always looking for the next great thing, the next encounter, the next achievement. Look around you. What do you love about what is already in your life? *Let's be more specific…*if you had to move tomorrow, what would you miss from your home, your current environment?

May 9

You can feel that you are entering a new moment of your life and that these releases are necessary for your highest good. This is powerful but uncomfortable. You may feel unstable or hesitant still. Don't let fear guide you. You can be this glorious, unapologetic version of you. Great times are ahead. You'll find the strength to permanently release what's not aligned anymore.

May 10

What's the last positive feedback or compliment that you received and really touched your heart? Can you remember what was said, and write it down below? What word was the most meaningful to you?

May 11

You don't have to know everything. You just have to feel good in this moment - to feel safe and protected. To feel self-loving. Find this sweet spot where you can both experience the unknown and maintain your grounding. Soon something that has felt confused, unstable, will be born again in full light and full clarity. Hold on. The path is being shown.

May 12

Picture yourself at a younger age, say between 15 and 18. What did you envision for your romantic relationships to be later in life? To what extent things are conform or different from what you envisioned?

May 13

You are not only this moment, your doubts, or choices to make. You are much more and much bigger. The mission…Your calling. Your unique golden path. A moment of connection between past and future. Feel your strength, your *power*. All is in divine order. You are experiencing the rewards of the seeds you planted during many, many Moons. Take the bird-eye view. Everything is a journey. Your power is growing, amplifying as you go.

May 14

What's your favorite way to slow down and relax? Can you bring more of this in your life for the next seven days?

May 15

A portal of massive shift in consciousness is opening. You can expect a turnaround in your emotions, your heart, and your thoughts. This cosmic phase is helping you reaffirm your sovereignty and implement the next step of your highest path. Nothing happening now is random. All is here to make you evolve. Your consciousness is experiencing an accelerated jump forward. Be moved.

May 16

Today, let's express a nice compliment or very positive feedback to a colleague at work. Or if you don't currently work, or work from home, let's express some very positive feedback to somebody within your very close relationships (family, friends), or your entourage (neighbor, shopkeeper from a store you're used to going to). It feels so good to give! Often in life, we give only when we know we'll receive back. But we learn that the more we give, the more we receive. Love is like a flow, and we all are canals for its expression. How did expressing positive feedback made you feel?

May 17

A full recalibration of your body and spirit is still downloading during these post-Eclipse days. Close relationships are at the forefront. You are invited to feel what's acceptable for you now, what is not, and what you truly want. Change starts with you. You set the tone of everything else around you by asserting your boundaries and daring your limits. The status quo can't remain. Trust your guidance and keep facing forward, one step after the next.

May 18

Today let me know, what's your favorite work of art (poem, painting, sculpture, novel, architecture) and why? What does this say about you?

May 19

Something new is opening. You may feel called in a different direction, but at the same time there is a void feeling - as if you were awaiting a confirmation. Just allow a little more time to sort things out. Be the chalice, the cosmic attractor, solidly anchored in your highest self. Something has been released, and forward movement is inevitable now.

May 20

Can you remember the best romantic night that you had in the past? Pick only one, and bask in this energy for a little while!

May 21

You are reaching a new place of inner balance. You are feeling fresh, energized, ready to follow through with your vision. A hopeful and action oriented energy is reaching you. You will get where you are aiming at. Start giving real momentum to these things that matter the most to you now. You are immensely supported.

May 22

Have you felt that you may have intuitive or clairvoyant gifts? Are you for instance drawn to Tarot cards, or perhaps you feel you are able to read other people aura's colors? Or maybe you feel a sacred connection to some places, and feel their energy? Perhaps you feel you can communicate with those who passed? Now if so, is it something you'd like to grow?

____

____

____

____

____

May 23

You are on the verge of making big changes and taking real forward action in the physical. Center yourself. Find your clarity, find your strength. You know what you have to do. You know what's the highest path. Trust yourself, and a little more. Your expansion into this new version of yourself is your birthright.

____

____

____

____

____

May 24

We all have comfort foods we go to when feeling a need of a rapid boost or soft, loving energy. What are yours? Do you go to chocolate, cookies or would you rather enjoy a burger in such cases? List your favorite comfort foods below and describe when you feel drawn to each of them.

____

____

____

____

____

____

May 25

What an intense May we have moved through. So much has been under shaking energy and turbulences, including relationships. In your heart, a decision was made. Maybe a difficult one. Like a revelation, or a turning point that won't go backwards. This is already manifesting physical change, whether you see it or not. Continue. A new energy is born from within you. You have changed. Your new phase is finding solid ground.

____

____

____

____

May 26

What was the best moment today? What happened? Try to recall the beautiful emotions and sensations you felt at that time! Keep them a little more with you.

____

____

____

____

May 27

Your energy feels like it is coming back online. You are at last ready to take action, more than before. It is like a boost from the Universe, reawakening the inner fire. You are finally about to see some changes take place. It is getting real. Keep going. Nothing can stop your inner resolve from moving forward toward this new room of experiences.

____

____

____

____

May 28

Today will be a long-term mission for you, if you accept it! Start a gratitude journal. Every time something beautiful happens to you, whether it is the result from your work or the energy you dedicated to something, or a totally unexpected gift from the Universe, write about it! Even the "small" blessings are to be written there. Keep track. You are so blessed. Make all the magic you receive count. The more grateful you are, the more you'll receive!

____

____

____

____

May 29

Your reality is changing. Life is sending you an opportunity to get closer to something you longed for. You are allowing yourself to step into a new timeline. Keep moving forward even if not everybody gets to where you are right now. You will meet more of your tribe as you go. Major soul connections are on the other side of the leap.

____

____

____

____

____

May 30

What's your biggest sexual fantasy? If you're in a relationship, are you comfortable with sharing this with your person/partner?

____

____

____

____

____

May 31st

Tomorrow will be a joyful, inspiring, successful day. What's the one thing you don't want to miss or absolutely want to do tomorrow?

Conclusion for May:

As we are reaching May's completion, you may find it interesting to ask yourself:

- What did you learn about yourself this month?

- Which prompt did you find the most challenging?

- Which prompt was the most enlightening to you, made you discover something about yourself or shifted the way you see things?

- Now that the month is over, and from what you've learned and written, is there a new action you'd like to take to upgrade your life for the best?

"We seek power and validation outside
of ourselves in many different ways,
until we find it within.
YOU, you are the only Yes to your full
expression that you need."

Sophie Gregoire, "She is the Moon"

June

June 1

There is something that you can't deny anymore. It is a need of yours, a want. Something that must happen for you, your path. For the pursuit of your destiny. Make a move now if you are ready, later if you are not. Divine timing is at play, as always. You will know when it is time. But don't let go of truth anymore. Truth needs you. Life needs you in your highest form.

June 2

If there is one thing you would like to do or complete this month, what would that be? Write this down! Start by taking a small step toward your goal!

____

____

____

____

June 3

This Eclipse window has been like a storm for many. Something was permanently released, changed, or truth came up, often in intense and unexpected ways. Give this a little rest for the moment. Breathe in a little more joy. Your process is still unfolding even when things aren't dramatic or crazy. What you seek seeks you too. Come back to inner harmony. Trust.

____

____

____

____

June 4

I'm sure you have a person in your life that understands and knows you better than anyone else. Or maybe, if you are lucky, you have two! Who is this person? How did it happen that they have learned so much about you?

____

____

____

____

____

June 5

What can't continue as it is being shown? You can't move forward in that same way. Trust your body. You have tried, you have given energy, you have compromised your needs or let the unacceptable install itself. It is time to respond differently. To take better care of yourself. Your limit zone has been reached. Trust. A new path is being shown.

____

____

____

____

____

June 6

"Your core values are the deeply held beliefs that authentically describe your soul."

— John C. Maxwell

Our values are the ideas we hold to be important. Defining our values helps us build a compass for our lives. Something that will help orient ourselves, make decisions. Today, try to list three of your most important values. One way to do that is to go back to previous experiences that felt really good - where you truly felt alive and engaged - and see what the underlying value was. You can also think of people that you admire, and try to identify what value(s) seem to describe their experience of life. All right, you may also read the list below and choose your top five values!

- Authenticity
- Achievement
- Adventure
- Authority
- Autonomy
- Balance
- Beauty
- Boldness
- Compassion
- Challenge
- Citizenship
- Community
- Competency
- Contribution
- Creativity
- Curiosity
- Determination
- Fairness
- Faith
- Fame
- Friendships
- Fun
- Growth
- Happiness
- Honesty

- Humor
- Influence
- Inner Harmony
- Justice
- Kindness
- Knowledge
- Leadership
- Learning
- Love
- Loyalty
- Meaningful Work
- Openness
- Optimism
- Peace
- Pleasure
- Poise
- Popularity
- Recognition
- Religion
- Reputation
- Respect
- Responsibility
- Security
- Self-Respect
- Service
- Spirituality
- Stability
- Success
- Status
- Trustworthiness

- Wealth
- Wisdom

*List Source: James Clear's website, Core Values List: Over 50 Common Personal Values (jamesclear.com).

June 7

Expect karma to be restored. To receive more of the energy that you've sowed. Expect the foundations of your life to be upgraded for the best.

June 8

Let's speak of your past a little bit today. We all have such things, "unfinished business" as they say. People we didn't say a proper goodbye to. Projects we didn't complete. Ideas we released, while still thinking of them often. What from your past feels unresolved?

June 9

Nothing wrong happens when you express to yourself how you truly feel. Nothing breaks. You are fine. By listening, you become more intimate with yourself. You get closer to you. You offer the possibility of change a stable ground. Allow the gateways within to open. Allow the tides to flow.

June 10

This is going to be a longer assignment for today. Deeper too. Take the version of you from 10 years ago. Write her/him a loving, encouraging, supportive letter. What advice could you give them from your current perspective, now that you know more?

June 11

For a moment of joy, pause. Let go of anxiety, worry and fear. Give this part of things a rest. Auspicious cosmic energy is available. Go with it. Do what makes you feel good, what ignites the spark of joy within your heart, your soul. Follow the goals that give you more life, more hope. You haven't arrived, yet you are advanced enough to enjoy what's available to you now. It's already big enough. Receive.

June 12

Today, let's give a call or send a text to someone that matters to you but that you usually don't have the time to reach out to. Give them some recent news and ask how they are doing.

June 13

Suppressed emotions could be resurfacing at this time. Listen. Allow. This is how you are finding your way forward. The Universe is never against you. Even when circumstances test you to the ultimate degree. You are strong enough to get closer to your calling, even if this involves an ending. The night always precedes sunrise. Don't let the idea of pain block your way. You are held. You never know what could find you after a leap of faith.

____

____

____

____

____

June 14

Is there any belief you were raised with, or that you witnessed within your family line, that you now disagree with? Why?

____

____

____

____

June 15

It has been months since you have tried to move the energy in a direction. Success after test - you didn't give up. Sometimes, you kept moving even if everything around you was nebulous, unclear, or even against it. You were stronger than the obstacles. Higher than was what directly in front of you. Keep going. Your path is assured. Your success is under way. All is progressing well. The completion of a phase of patient effort is around the corner. Be proud.

____

____

____

____

June 16

"A flower blossoms for its own joy."

— Oscar Wilde

Have you ever done something that was truly important to you, even if you weren't supported by your people? Have you ever wanted something so bad that you had to confront opposition to get there, and maybe even disengage from some groups or friendships to follow your own calling? What was that? Are you proud you did so?

____

____

____

____

June 17

Time for a very powerful Full Moon in the days which surround this forecast. This will mark the transition into the happier rest of the year. This is a shift of energy. Your vibration is being lifted. Keep moving forward. You are right before receiving something big.

June 18

Today, take some time to look at your physical image in the mirror and hold yourself in love. See the beauty. Observe it, take your time. Look at your face, your eyes, your hair, your arms. Practice observing your image with tenderness and love. You are beautiful.

June 19

Your life is upgrading rapidly. You are moving forward at a fast pace, completely releasing old cycles. More fear was released out of your system. You are following your intuition, feeling so much more confident as you pursue the call of your name. Light codes are poured onto you. Receive.

June 20

Hello! Just wondering, what motivated you to get out of bed this morning?

June 21

A strong and light energy is being sent to you. You are reawakening a beautiful, almost innocent, inner joy and hope for life after months of turbulence. Since January, you have made big decisions for yourself. You retrieved some of your power. You adapted fast to change. Now abundance wants to find you. Believe. All the seeds you planted will hatch out. Your dreams will come true.

____

____

____

June 22

What is the biggest pain or heartbreak you felt in your life? How did you overcome it? What did you learn?

____

____

____

____

____

June 23

The Solstice energy is implementing. You are experiencing another upgrade. The transformation you are experiencing is big. It's taking off of you all the energies, within and without, which could hinder your highest expansion. Blocks are removed. Your inner attractor is changing. Don't go back to old ways or fears. Your life is improving for the best.

____

____

____

____

June 24

When I say the word "love," who is the first person that comes to mind? Why?

June 25

Some of your deepest soul desires could become true sooner than you think. The hard work is about to pay off. It has already done so behind the scenes. Sometimes months or years of inner work, of truly seeing your value, lead to a specific point of ultimately breaking through. You are close to a point of major karmic turnaround, a point when destiny and soul plan are fulfilled.

June 26

Are there any social issues you are passionate about? Diversity? Women's rights? Fight against domestic violence? Animal welfare? Environmental issues? Work pressure and burn out? Money inequality?

What are you doing about them? Is there something you could invest yourself deeper in?

____

____

____

____

____

June 27

A huge influx of light is being received. Causing important waves of emotions, almost uncontrollable, as well as truths being revealed or significant plot twists. Hang in there. Let the flow move you, while not becoming it. You are more than what shifts and turns. You are the continuation of your own soul plan, always progressing - always transforming and releasing in the name of your highest transmutation and your most sacred becoming.

____

____

____

____

June 28

Let's travel back to your childhood years. What were your dreams as a child? Do you feel that you're fulfilling them?

____

____

____

____

_____________________________________J

une 29

You are leaving an old version of you behind. It's done. You may not recognize yourself or your reactions now that you've passed the threshold. It may feel awkward, but you're healing so much. Walk forward in peace.

____

____

____

____

June 30

Big question for today! Pablo Picasso said, "The meaning of life is to find your gift. The purpose of life is to give it away." Do these words resonate? Do you feel that you have found your "gift" – the unique magic that's only yours and no one else's? This can be anything! Truly, there are no rules.

____

____

____

____

Conclusion for June:

As we are reaching June's completion, you may find it interesting to ask yourself:

- What did you learn about yourself this month?

- Which prompt did you find the most challenging?

- Which prompt was the most enlightening to you, made you discover something about yourself or shifted the way you see things?

- Now that the month is over, and from what you've learned and written, is there a new action you'd like to take to upgrade your life for the best?

"There is nothing more rare, more beautiful, than a woman being unapologetically herself, comfortable in her perfect imperfection. To me, that is the true essence of beauty."

Steve Maraboli

July

*"July is tender. Part nostalgic and part wild. The raw
flesh of the summer".*
—**Victoria Erickson**

July 1

The energy is sensitive. What is shifting is deep. You are retrieving
more of your power. A lot can flourish and manifest this July.
Dreams want to come true. Keep going. So much misalignment
has been washed away.

July 2

Today, let's do something super fun. You're going to change your first name! I hope you'll have an opportunity to do this today. For instance, if you give your name for some email newsletters, a loyalty card or even at a coffee place, let's change it! You have ever dreamt of bearing the name Lola? Choose it? You want to have even more fun? Tell the barista your name is Forever Golden or Cat Lover, or Magic Beauty… Be creative!

July 3

You have received massive light downloads in the past days and may have taken a leap, or you are preparing to take one. This is important change, and a key "rising" on your life path and soul journey. There won't be a way back from this elevation, from this state. This change is deep, a reconnection to your inner knowing, and to a higher form of personal power. Keep going. Very old inner blocks have been removed from your field.

July 4

We are living lives that are so busy. From morning to night, there is something to do. Sometimes, we feel that we need to be productive to feel good. We need to tick all the items of our to-do list to be happy and proud of our day. Are we, as humans, a number of tasks? Is one's value defined by their productivity? Today, you'll do completely different. Let's take one item off your to-do list. Let's postpone it to later, for once in a while! It's good to do exactly the opposite of what we're expected to do.

____

____

____

____

____

July 5

Triggers are helping you shed layers and grow into a higher version of you. More aligned, more free. Your path and recent changes are directed by your spirit, your soul. Let go of the contraction. Forgive yourself for the "mistakes" in this time of great expansion. Continue allowing this new energy to move you, while being extremely gentle with yourself. What you are doing needs bravery. What you are doing needs self-love and self-honoring.

____

____

____

____

July 6

This is summer! Make a list of all your favorite things about this season. If you're in the Southern Hemisphere, do the same. Make a list of all that you love about the rainy season, or the winter one.

____

____

____

____

____

July 7

The changes currently taking place are so important, so divine, so key. You are reconnecting with your higher self. You are allowing completely new pathways to bloom. You are allowing new answers to old issues. Life is shifting. Congratulate yourself. You found within yourself the bravery to create a new start.

____

____

____

____

____

July 8

Write a list of the five people from your past that you'd love to see again the most. What would you tell them?

____

____

____

____

____

____

July 9

This change is powerful but bringing anxiety. A part of you still wonders, subconsciously, if you can make it. Be strong. Believe in you. Pay less and less attention to the energies that disrupt you, don't see you, or are not on your side. The only thing that matters is that you are on the side of You, your biggest supporter.

____

____

____

____

July 10

When was the last time you took a risk? How did you overcome fear? Eventually, was the leap worth it?

____

____

____

____

July 11

This incoming New Moon is allowing your big transformation to reach a step, a zone, an area of stability. Emotions can feel intense, unstable. Let it flow. You are on the right track. Focus on self-care and just continuing.

July 12

Is there somebody you greatly admire? That can be a real person or a fictional hero. What in them truly inspires you? List three qualities that they have and that caused this draw for you.

July 13

You may currently need a lot of alone time to regroup and find yourself again, in the midst of this vortex of change. You must fulfil this need in order to hear yourself clearly. Misunderstandings with others may grow as some may not understand your new self, support, or connect with your current moves. Those meant

to stick with you will anyhow. Find peace and direction within.
The rest is secondary right now.

____

____

____

____

____

July 14

Co-creation is understanding that we are working in tandem
with the Universe to create our dream life. Co-creation means
two things. One, to not be too specific in what you order from
the Universe! For instance, if one is trying to attract a soulmate
in their lives, it's better to not be too narrowed about one specific
person, an ex, or somebody we are obsessing on. It's best to be open
to limitless possibilities and let the Universe surprise them, while
already feeling that love is in their lives. In other words, acting *as
if.* Secondly, co-creation means allowing the seeds we just planted
some time to grow – instead of always pushing, forcing, asking,
doing even. See, when you plant something. It takes time to hatch
out, and it takes time to get some flowers. Co-creation is like nature
– it asks of you to trust that with some water and sun, the idea
you planted one day will become a tree. Long story short, keep
taking action toward your goals – water this seed, do what has to
be done, give it some sun, but don't obsess about it. Let it be and
grow. Allow some room for the Universe to give the most perfect
color it wants it to have for you. Allow life to meet you halfway.

So…how do you feel about this? Is this something you practice in your life?

July 15

Your world is changing. Relationship dynamics are redefined as you are seeing more clearly where you have given your power away. Your wellbeing is once again the priority for you, even in relationship containers. In fact, you are the one in charge of defining the boundaries or lines that others can't go past. It is about how you use your time, your energy. How you let the ways of others affect you. Your confidence is increasing and allowing you to reach for new heights, new joy, new opportunities. Make the most of this time. The sky is the limit.

July 16

Hey, let's set your mind to travelling again! Create a list of the places you dream of visiting. Don't be shy! We want some of these trips to open up your mind to new worlds and possibilities.

July 17

The energy is back again to a more yellow, golden tone. You have strengthened yourself. Less external things can affect you as you walk in the direction of you, of your dream, of your highest self. Keep going, anchored in yourself, understanding that other people's responses to your growth are a projection of their own path and the way they feel about themselves. Observe. Pay attention only to what truly matters to you. The continuation of your path is your priority.

July 18

"The journey not the arrival matters." T. S. Eliot

Does this idea resonate with you? Generally speaking in your life, are you more into living and experiencing the journey, or reaching a destination or goal?

July 19

The year hasn't been easy for many so far. We have been through significant Tower moments, especially in the past two months. Let go of force. Let go of the questions. Be willing to let life lead you. Trust life enough to be ready to give her the reins at this time, for a little while. You need rest. You need peace. You need to forgive self and others. You need to trust life and others, one more time.

July 20

If you were to take a little more care of your body, what would you do differently today?

July 21

The Leo season is on approach. You are starting to feel new vibes of personal rising. New opportunities are taking shape as you allow yourself to take the steps and move toward renewal. Major milestones could be achieved this August. Major connections could form. Keep letting go of old blocks and stories, and embrace freely what brings joy. Be the writer of your own life. Choose the scenario and situations that give you so much contentment and fulfilment.

July 22

Have you already experienced feeling guided in your life? This could be noticing the Universe is presenting omens and synchronicities to you, as if showing a way. Or, this could be making a big and even challenging decision and feeling supported every step of the way, as if the Universe was there telling you "I see you, fellow wanderer. I support you." Also sometimes, we utterly want something and the Universe keeps seemingly refusing our request. It is like one's wish is never granted. Often, after a few months or years, one understands why this happened that way – it makes sense. There was something better for them, better than what they thought was optimal. That's another way of the Universe to guide souls –

by redirecting them toward a path that's for the highest good. So, have you already experienced receiving guidance from the Universe, a higher power, or something greater than you? If so, share below about your experience.

____

____

____

____

____

July 23

An old self is currently being released. You are moving toward things that are out of your comfort zone, but you are ready. In some way, you have been prepping for this time for years. In some way, what's happening now is simply the result of so many efforts, work and shedding. You manifested this new timeline all the way. Congratulate yourself for this new dawn. Keep going. A new territory is calling you.

____

____

____

____

July 24

Do you consider yourself more like a lone wolf or a team player? Or does this vary? What's your favorite role among the two? Write a few lines below!

____

____

____

____

July 25

New positive experiences are headed your way. A heaviness has been washed away. Shine, warrior. New physical manifestations of your power are taking shape. New dreams are taking form in your heart. Those are important. Your energy is moving higher, free from old obstacles.

____

____

____

____

July 26

What's the outfit of yours that feels the most aligned with you, your essence, your spirit? Why? Is it its colors, or its shape? The way it makes you feel? Its energy? Write a few lines below.

____

____

____

____

____

July 27

The Lion's gate portal is now open. You may have felt stuck or limited in your ability to align with tangible blessings lately, and to truly see your physical reality upgrade - but this energy of shedding, cleansing, and even overthinking is about to reach an ending. Your energy is undergoing a recalibration. Things will feel different in a couple of weeks time. As always, August comes with the promise of changes, discovery, and sudden leaps into a bigger embodiment of your own unique soul power. New codes are going to be received in the next few days. Receive this new light. Allow your vision to expand. Allow yourself a new glow.

____

____

____

____

July 28

A human's memory works in different ways. Some people's memories are almost only images, like pictures of the past. Some are carried back to old days through specific meals or scents. Some others feel a lot when hearing music they used to listen to. Can you remember the music of your childhood? List some of your favorite songs and tunes from the good old days.

July 29

You are flying out of the caterpillar mode - now a butterfly and not chrysalis anymore. The guidance is strong. You may still hesitate, but at each crossroads, big or small, you can feel which path is the one of expansion. This is not fear. This is excitement. Your soul is ready for more. You may be experiencing an expansion of your gifts and imagine a whole new spectrum for your mission. Some of these dreams and goals have been awaiting your readiness, for months and for years. This is a whole new level. Don't dim your light. Keep blossoming.

July 30

We all have great moments in our lives that we are immensely proud of, even years after. These specific moments, events, achievements, or days – are key for the progressive construction of our identity. They are like "roles of a lifetime." Could you recall one of these founding moments that you had? Write a few lines about it below. Try and remember some saucy details!

July 31

You are leaving an old version of you behind. It's done. You may not recognize yourself or your reactions fully now that you've passed the threshold. It may feel awkward but you're healing so much. Walk forward in peace.

Conclusion for July:

As we are reaching July's completion, you may find it interesting to ask yourself:

- What did you learn about yourself this month?

- Which prompt did you find the most challenging?

- Which prompt was the most enlightening to you, made you discover something about yourself or shifted the way you see things?

- Now that the month is over, and from what you've learned and written, is there a new action you'd like to take to upgrade your life for the best?

"If you can, if you're able to. Don't fall in love with a person's potential. Who they could be, who they could have been – who they could have risen, soared into.

If you can, and even if you see the purity of a soul – fall in love with a person. Fall in love with a man or a woman. Words, flesh, actions. Actual beingness, actual behavior."

Sophie Gregoire, "She is the Moon"

August

"August of another summer, and once again
I am drinking the sun
and the lilies again are spread across the water."
— **Mary Oliver**

August 1

This time may feel intense, *big*. So much light seeks to enter your system and is pushing the old ways out. A lot of emotional trauma healing can be expected at this time as the energy tries to reach a space as cleansed as possible. Allow yourself to digest it step by step. Remember that all clearings are the pathway to more light.

August 2

Today, write a letter to someone you love, living or dead. Write them what's in your heart, share your heart, your feelings. Express your gratitude!

August 3

Waves of ancestral lineage wounds are coming up for more healing. You are strong. You have awareness. You always have the power to change the storyline.

August 4

If you could instantly change one thing about yourself with a unicorn magic wand, what would that be?

August 5

Your fire is lit up. You will never dim your light or abandon yourself these same ways any longer. You are your own savior. King and Priestess. Sacred defender of your own fire. By embodying your own role in the grand scheme of things, embodying fully your own power, you help us all. You heal us all. You inhabit your own space in the grand patchwork. See big possibilities. You are powerful. Your vision is your birthright.

August 6

Today, you have done magical things. You accomplished some work, of whatever kind. You may have received acknowledgment from others for this. Maybe you haven't. Maybe they were too busy, or couldn't see your work and efforts fully with their eyes. So, for all the things you did today, and you'd like to receive recognition and gratitude for, give this directly to yourself. You deserve acknowledgement.

August 7

The energy is agitated. Strong. Intense. You may be finding yourself in initiation-type situations right now. The influx of light is very present but the birth of more always comes with a sort of "moving through," of rite of passage. The energy is speeding up. A deeper layer of your light is trying to hatch out. Deeper layers of your service to the world are trying to rise.

August 8

This morning, as you start your day, plan to come back home tonight with a little special thing for each of the people who live with you. A postcard, a flower, a magazine, anything…even a simple gesture. If you currently live on your own, plan to bring something back to someone you often see in your life (at work, or a friend, or a lover…). Make them smile!

August 9

The Lion's Gate portal is now wide open. This is a very potent doorway. Miracles and big realizations could happen. In all cases intuitive nudges will be very powerful and guide you along the next level of your sacred path. Ground. Prepare yourself to receive a big influx of light. A new, deeper part of your inner power is activated.

____

____

____

____

August 10

What's something that happened in recent weeks, which possibly hurt you, and that you haven't forgiven yet? Do you feel that it's something you could eventually forgive? How would that feel?

____

____

____

____

August 11

New energy is coming in and old energy is leaving. Your approach to things is changing. A lot has been cleared energetically very recently. New mission or relationship blueprints are being born. It is now time for integration. Allow new energy to take shape within you. Be patient as magic unfolds.

____

____

____

____

____

August 12

Today, share about the person you see today as your best friend. We want you to choose somebody that has stood the test of time with you, not somebody too recent in your life. What do you appreciate about them and this connection? Why is it working? Why does it last?

____

____

____

____

____

August 13

You may see yourself experiencing old situations in a new way. Confronted again to the same old stories but responding differently, finding a new way. Generational trauma is cleared deeper. You are seeing more of your subconscious limitations, releasing more of them, and gaining more conscious sovereignty of your life. Trust. You are breaking through.

August 14

What is the last compliment you remember giving?

August 15

Lots of physical symptoms, especially since the Lion's Gate. Real rest is required. Hang in there. You are being prepared for your next level. Bigger is coming.

August 16

How would you like to be seen by those closest to you? Which adjectives would you like to hear from them to describe you?

August 17

You are working every day, consistently, at building a future that's aligned with who you have become. Your forces feel redirected toward new endeavors, new manifestations. You are courageous and daring, called by what must happen now, what should unfold for the highest good of all. Your bravery is seen. Keep going. You are on your way to an even higher You.

August 19

What a big August we are having. So many shifts, changes of directions, and releasing of emotions we thought were gone. You are slowly moving out the womb space and into the rebirth. This is not the time to give up on your recent resolve. Soon you will feel out of this decision-making or introspective mode and be reborn into a new space of clarity and purpose. You were right to take those leaps. Believe in yourself. Believe in what's guiding you.

August 20

Do you see yourself as lucky or unlucky in love? Why?

August 21

In the next 24 hours and as we get closer to the Full Moon, (Aquarius) blocks are about to be removed. Clarity is coming back. You know what you have to do in the name of your true self.

A new timeline is available if you are brave enough to follow your heart's calling. You are shaping your reality through your courage. The old is leaving.

August 22

In romantic relationships, there are things that we can compromise about in order to allow the relationship flourish, or because we are learning from our partners. Sometimes, we are initially embarrassed by something that the relationship is asking of ourselves, only to later discover that we actually evolved in a positive way through it. But sometimes it is the opposite – it's what some call the *"non-negotiables."* What are these for you?

____

____

____

____

____

August 23

You have been through all the shifts, all the transformation pressure, and now new horizons are making themselves known to you. You are rediscovering that you are totally allowed to be yourself fully, authentically, in your own unique and out-of-the-box way. Break the molds. Break the old ways. You are free.

____

____

____

____

August 24

What kind of relationships would you like to develop over the next six months or year? Very close friendships? Social circle and acquaintances? Family? Business partnerships? Romantic ones?

August 25

Things may have felt chaotic since July. Some were forced to break down, or to feel inner dark parts so that a real letting go can happen. The invitation is to own reality and truth fully, and to forge a new path. You can do this. Dare newness. Things have changed. Your freedom of now may look different than it used to be. Being in your power may look different, too. You can decide to show up for yourself as you need it now. Have the courage to feel who you are now, and what's happening. Move forward accordingly.

August 26

What is the area of your life (love, career, creativity, friendships, health, wealth, family) that you would like to see upgraded in a year, if you had to choose just one?

____

____

____

____

August 27

A major release of heavy energy is reaching completion. You may need a little more time, and a little more space, to get ready. Give yourself what you need. Nourish yourself. Things aren't as daunting as they recently felt. The Heart Chakra is reopening.

____

____

____

____

August 28

> *"Sometimes the only available transportation is a leap of faith"*
>
> — Margaret Shepard.

How does this make you feel? Do you agree? Have you ever applied this belief to your life?

August 29

After a time of processing, inner work, facing and releasing shadows - you may feel like you are coming out of a storm. The light is coming back. You are ready to start again. To dive in life fully again as a new energy has arrived. You were waiting for a new start - and this time has come now. Things are finding a place of greater light and ease. You may also feel less in the dark and so more willing to do what makes you happy. Do your work of joy. Great unfolding is so close now.

August 30

Today, let's make one promise to yourself about something that matters to you. Hold yourself to it!

August 31

It feels that something is about to happen. As if the new dawn still hasn't fully shown up. As if more awaits. As if the rebirth hadn't fully spoken its name. Keep integrating the light energy. Rest, and when life force is present, follow your own Sun.

Conclusion for August:

As we are reaching August's completion, you may find it interesting to ask yourself:

- What did you learn about yourself this month?

- Which prompt did you find the most challenging?

- Which prompt was the most enlightening to you, made you discover something about yourself or shifted the way you see things?

- Now that the month is over, and from what you've learned and written, is there a new action you'd like to take to upgrade your life for the best?

"Whoever is happy will make others happy."

Anne Frank

September

"Autumn, you remind me of past lovers. You remind me of what's gone. You remind me of poetry."
— **Sophie Gregoire**

September 1

You are recommitting to yourself. Embracing your authentic self deeper, telling them a bigger "Yes. I believe in you." As if another layer of external influences had been shed. You are letting go of more fear and stepping with bravery in the path of your personal rising. You are ready to take steps to be in the world of those things that you have yearned for within. Keep going. More magic is about to manifest as you get closer to the path of the authentic you.

September 2

Your sacred space. We all have a sacred space, which is simply and basically a place, a room, a cushion or a specific location that makes us feel good. It is a place or environment (having a bunch of crystals around or carrying our favorite necklace) that helps us create an atmosphere of safety and calmness for ourselves. It is a set of circumstances that helps feeling grounded and connected to a form of higher power. So what do you personally need to create your sacred space? Is it a specific place? Objects you need to have with you? A way you like to be seated? Reflect on this and write your thoughts below!

September 3

There is something you have been contemplating for a while now, like a major decision, and the fog is now clearing and you are ready to make an interesting change. Whatever that is, it is about embracing your true nature more. Last week you may have fallen into old ways, confusion and doubts, may have even have experienced some Tower moments where you were forced to face the truth. A resistance is collapsing within you now. It is a big release. You are ready to let go of a burden. Allow it. Be guided by the sound of rebirth that's awaiting on the other side.

September 4

Today, dress yourself in a way that makes you feel you, authentically you. And confident. You are unique. You are golden. Be proud of who you are.

September 5

Something about this energy is entirely new. You have never felt before that you could overcome so many obstacles. You have never felt that you could free yourself from all these blocks, these thoughts. Keep going. You are walking unapologetically towards the life that was made for you.

____

____

____

____

September 6

What's the movie that inspired you the most, and why? Share a little about this below.

____

____

____

____

September 7

You are setting a new path for yourself. The Leo's season may have reawakened the spark within - lit again the fire of your authentic self, your self-expression, your creativity, and your voice. This Virgo season allows you to take the steps that will support this big vision into existence. Expansion and broadening your own horizon are so potent right now. Take that new course. Connect with this new social circle. Ground your big ideas into the first steps of their reality. You are manifesting.

____

____

____

____

____

September 8

Birthdays can be truly magical. Some are better than others, however. In fact, some of our birthdays are connected with less happy times or memories in our lives. Some were better, maybe because we had a soul mate or so many of our loved ones around. Can you recall your most magical birthday? Write about it below!

____

____

____

____

September 9

Magical portal 9/9. You may be feeling in-between worlds. Your energy is trying to move past blockages and then it may be tempted to move backwards, unsure. You are being recalibrated. Every time you go beyond something that would have previously stopped you, and you allow the expression of the natural flow that moves from within, you are on the right track.

____

____

____

____

September 10

What is your relationship with parenthood? If you are a parent, reflect on how this deeply transformed you, and how. If you are not, is that something you desire? Something you would have liked to be different? Or is the fact of not having children, at least so far, a deliberate choice?

September 11

New codes and templates have been activated within you. With this comes the completion, and the end of a cycle, of an old you. Finding more of your soul power also means that you can't be the same as before anymore. You are being shown a new way. New opportunities are coming as you are finding the strength to express a new you.

September 12

What was the most magical time of your life? Remember, and then write a few lines below!

____

____

____

____

____

September 13

The energetics right now are teaching about patience, and slow and steady movement. You have all the ingredients and codes within yourself to envision and tap into the reality you want to create for yourself in the months to come. The vision board is clear. You have downloaded everything. And now, you are progressing one step after the other. Without force, but with receptivity and grace. You are moving forward incorporating both the Masculine & Feminine principles: a mix between deliberate action and allowing your seeds to grow, and your blessings to organically find you.

____

____

____

____

____

September 14

What was your favorite trip ever? Why? Remember it, what happened, how you felt. Write a few lines below!

____

____

____

____

September 15

You have put change energy in motion and now life is moving itself to meet you halfway. Things are happening behind the scenes. Your vision is supported. You will witness evidence of it. You are recommitting to what joy and power mean to you. The changes you are making now will serve you long-term. It is a karmic clearing.

____

____

____

____

September 16

Let's express some gratitude today. Share below three things you have achieved since the start of September, and three things you have learned since the beginning of the month, too. I'm sure you have a lot to share below!

September 17

You are being asked to take a step back and allow things to unfold. You have started to move the energy in new directions, and now your task is to stay on the same line and to trust. Surrender more. Allow more beauty to unfold on its own. Play more with the principle of grace. You are divinely supported. Now is not the time to force movement, but to allow your seeds to grow. All is well.

September 18

"Freedom is not the absence of commitments, but the ability to choose - and commit myself to - what is best for me."

— Paulo Coelho.

What does freedom mean to you? Is freedom a complete lack of attachments and obligations, or of long-term plans? Or is freedom the possibility to actually create and design our own path as we please, even if we become builders, solidly anchored in a community, family, work or life mission?

What are your thoughts?

September 19

The energetics have been intense in the past 48 hours. There is a sense of not knowing anymore who you are and what your true goal is. Mental confusion may be present. Disturbed sleep or strange, vivid dreams or nightmares are common right now. Our bodies are trying to process the constant upgrades. If ascension symptoms are strong for you, know that this is going up until the Equinox and will dissolve after this step. The best you can do is take care of yourself, and your physical needs, and give yourself some down time.

September 20

Let's go to a more creative writing prompt! Start with "that evening"... and call back to your current awareness a memory.

Write what comes. Don't make it beautiful or pretty. Just remember. Immerse yourself in it, in the sensations, the feelings… Go back it time and let your hand flow on the paper.

____

____

____

____

September 21

A lot of this journey is actually about letting go. Old visions of your life, of yourself. Becoming what is right in your heart may be a stormy road, but it is the right path. Any phase of doubt leads to a deeper reclaiming of what is truth for you. This time is emotional. Be gentle and loving with yourself. You will come through.

____

____

____

____

September 22

"One does not become enlightened by imagining figures of light, but by making the darkness conscious."

— Carl Gustav Jung.

This quotation is a famous one. It's general and abstract. Can you give at least two examples of this process in your own life? When have you faced your shadows or fears, accepted to meet deeper parts of yourself, and then brought them back to awareness? How has this helped you?

____

____

____

____

September 23

This is an intense, almost impressive incoming Full Moon. Release energy is in the air. Take time for yourself even if it means changing your routine for a while. Focus on your inner peace and finding your center, even if this means doing nothing or following a new path of joy, of aliveness. Drop the obligations you do out of fear or to chase outcomes. You are given rebirth energy. Your rebirth is found in befriending yourself even more.

____

____

____

____

September 24

If you had a time machine, what is the one thing of your past that you would change and why? That can be an old or recent memory!

____

____

____

____

____

September 25

This Equinox is bringing a soft, slow magic. This is your cosmic opportunity to allow shifts to take place, mainly by letting go. Some things brought you joy, were elevating your life, or brought needed wisdom to your soul in the past, but part of this has changed. Some things were a match to former cycles, but have had their time and don't belong to where you are headed now. Find this soft quietness within, this loving silence who knows it all. Listen. You are readjusting your path for the best.

____

____

____

____

____

September 26

We haven't spoken that much about health so far! What are your health goals? What do you wish to change or improve? More exercise, a change in diet? Set yourself some realistic timelines to clearly define your goals!

____

____

____

____

____

September 27

Seven planetary bodies are currently in retrograde. It is a powerful moment of personal evolution as more old energy is coming back up to the surface to allow a grand rebirth. Allow the movement of the energy. Allow yourself to change your mind, see things differently, and to change the priorities in your life. Change is a constant for you. Important new insights are being revealed.

____

____

____

____

September 28

If you could choose one field that you could be an expert at, what would you choose, and why?

____

____

____

____

September 29

You are discovering more things that may not be in complete alignment with your authentic expression. It is a perfect time to let them go. Full alignment is a process. A journey. It is more than ok to keep finding who you are through discovering who you are not. You have the right to change. To transform. You have the right to let go.

____

____

____

____

September 30

Let's end September with a deep, profound question. Do you feel that you are living the life that you planned? Have you begun achieving the desires and goals you set for yourself a few years ago? Are you under pressure to be on the right track?

____

____

____

____

____

Conclusion for September:

As we are reaching September's completion, you may find it interesting to ask yourself:

- What did you learn about yourself this month?

- Which prompt did you find the most challenging?

- Which prompt was the most enlightening to you, made you discover something about yourself or shifted the way you see things?

- Now that the month is over, and from what you've learned and written, is there a new action you'd like to take to upgrade your life for the best?

"To live is the rarest thing in the world.
Most people just exist."

Oscar Wilde

October

"I'm so glad I live in a world where there are
Octobers."
— L. M. Montgomery, Anne of Green Gables

October 1

A lot is going on in your world. Physically, but also like a deeper dive within. Take some time for you. Allow this pause. Give yourself softness, love, and nurturing. Let go of the action steps for a moment. Your healing heart needs you.

October 2

What was the most terrifying experience of your life?

October 3

We are moving through a key moment of recalibration. Our physical and emotional bodies are moving through a reset to integrate the transformation. This time may feel intense and triggering. Boundaries with others are changing and can't go backwards, since we reclaimed more of our power. A rebirth is happening, and that's why these frictions are present. Continue focusing on the things and ways that represent the new energy for you, and let your world adjust accordingly.

October 4

If you could sum up this last month in one word, what would it be, and why? Share this below!

____

____

____

____

October 5

Powerful changes are ahead. You are greatly transforming. Energy ebbs and flows, but don't cancel the next beautiful forward moves that you have designed for yourself when you were feeling energized or called. Walk bravely through this. You called that in for such a long time. You deserve all the magic and success that's waiting on the other side of self-doubt. This isn't the time to give up.

____

____

____

____

October 6

Please express below two bad things that happened today (or yesterday, if it's morning for you) and two good ones.

____

____

____

____

October 7

It's been a while since the energy has not been that transforming. You are experiencing a restart. Things may be changing fast, but don't be scared. They only reflect your readiness. This time you are ready to give things a go, rather than beating around the bush as you might have done before. This is a time to embrace change, and to move bravely in the direction of the new opportunities around you. More of what you desire for your life is becoming accessible. This isn't chance. You called it in so many times. Be grateful for all the versions of yourself that did the work and led you to that point of now.

____

____

____

____

____

October 8

What's your favorite plant, flower or tree? What does it mean to you? How does it relate to your essence or personality?

____

____

____

____

October 9

There is a renewed sense of freedom in the air. Several planetary bodies are moving directly, and you are ready to implement change in a more stable and asserted way. You are seeing your old ways with fresh, empowered eyes, and you are willing to change the story. What was ok a few months ago isn't anymore. You are ready to do what it takes to be more of this more evolved version of you. You are transcending the ways that are outgrown. Be brave and follow through. You are embodying a new version of you.

____

____

____

____

____

October 10

Pick one person in your life that you think hates you. Prepare a speech for him/her. What would you say? What should they know? What haven't they understood about you?

____

____

____

____

____

October 11

Continuation of the 10/10 Portal. Rebirth energy. Feel the spirit of creation, new beginnings & an inner excitement. Like a page has been turned. Sovereignty codes abound. Feel your self-confidence rising. Receive.

____

____

____

____

____

October 12

Being on our own gives us the space we need to rest, relax, recover, and even heal. It helps us enjoy our own company. For some, it helps access their creative, artistic or intuitive gifts. We all have a different connection with "alone time." Some like a lot of it, others aren't comfortable with it and find it gloomy. What about you? What are five things you like doing when you are all by yourself?

____

____

____

____

October 13

Your transformation is well under way. The release of the old continues. If you can, pause for a while. See all that has changed this year. All you dared to see, to accomplish. Feel the beauty of your journey. You are strong. You keep letting go of the old and allowing new life to find you.

October 14

Write here all the things you ever wanted to tell an ex-partner. Anything. If there is pain, anger, guilt, whatever – it's good. Write it down. Write anything that come to mind. This is your space. Keep the paper/letter, or burn it – your choice. Go, go deep!

October 15

You are continuously adjusting to a new frequency. Each day comes with its tests, its softness, new pathways, and its rewards. You have changed within and you are organically anchoring this new frequency in your daily life. Something is relaxing on the inside, because you are softening into this new energy. Letting it take more space. It is a beautiful rebirth. There are many signs that you are on the right track.

October 16

What's the craziest thing you have ever done? That thing that surprised you the most about yourself? Share this below! And congrats, life finds its spark through these little crazy moves.

October 17

Be brave as we are riding the last wave of these retrogrades. You were pushed to let go of traits that weren't helping you be your highest form. You found the strength to redefine your path with a new-found awareness. Keep doing what's best for you now. Keep embracing what inspires. An old sense of self is gone and you are aligning with a new you. Be proud of yourself. You have done so much work this year.

October 18

Today, tell me about your morning. How do you wake up? What's in your breakfast? Do you have a morning routine? Do you take the car, walk to the bus stop, or walk to your work place? Be as specific as you can. Describe the tiny bits of it. Slow down the pace in your mind to recall the details of your morning.

October 19

Reminder…perhaps your voice, your art, won't speak to many, but it will speak a lot to those that it does. Don't seek quantity – seek what is true for you. Seek what flows freely from your soul.

October 20

Today, ask yourself…Is there something in your life that's not in alignment with who you truly are? By alignment, I mean something that's *not truly you.* Something that doesn't resonate with yourself, your personality, your joy, your soul. So, is there anything like that?

____

____

____

____

____

October 21

A new chapter is starting energetically for you. The puzzle is about to fall more and more into place after some time of heaviness, uncertainty, and perhaps difficulties in manifesting your vision fully. Allow a new sense of freedom to find you. Breathe deeply and absorb some fresh air.

____

____

____

____

____

October 22

Let me ask you, is there a specific pattern you feel that you have been repeating in your life for a while (for years, or even forever), but you wish you could avoid now? What is that? What's the thing you desire to respond to differently, to handle in a different way in the future?

October 23

There is a powerful Full Moon in Aries. You are reaching a higher level of awareness, permanently releasing behaviors and traits that were not helping you create the life that you want. Life is changing. Surrender. Powerful forces are at play. You are about to receive the harvest of all the efforts and deep work you did, as if in a cave, the last few months. Believe.

October 24

Oh my goodness, I adore this one! It's a great, great one! Today, let's imagine your life is a novel. The story of your life is a bestseller. What's the title of this book? Woohoo, let's be imaginative! Let's see big!

____

____

October 25

We are now entering both the Eclipse season and Scorpio season. Important truths are coming out of the shadows. You are ready to dive deeper in order to build your future in the most aligned ways. The right moves are coming into your awareness. Trust.

____

____

____

____

October 26

Today, let's dive into a little more powerful heart healing. You'll start by writing "I never got the chance to tell you any of this…", and see what comes. Who are you writing to? Let it flow. Let it be there with you. It's ok if tears come.

____

____

____

____

October 27

You've been through moments of chaos, significant revelations, and inner turmoil in the past few days. A deeper layer of your truth has been revealed. This may have been intense, but is for your highest good. Keep feeling what wants to be felt. Keep allowing new information to come up to your consciousness. You deserve everything your heart is whispering to you. A way will be found.

October 28

Today, grab a poetry book. Or find something online. Open to any page. Read a poem and choose the line you like the most. Why do you like this one specifically? Why does it resonate with you?

October 29

Even if this time has been intense, you know it was key for your path forward. Those changes in your inner world are important. They mark the start of a major opening. Something that was blocking your movement has been removed. Be hopeful. Have faith in your dreams. Feel this deep in your cells. Allow the Universe to take care of the details. It will meet you halfway.

____

____

____

____

____

October 30

Ok, it's almost the end of October. List below the three things that happened this month which you feel the most grateful for!

____

____

____

____

October 31

You are having a new awareness. It is something big. Out of your pain, a new vastness is re-emerging. Your path can continue, only with the attachments that are necessary. You are making room. You are ready to let go to an extent that allows you to see and to open new doors. Your path is in your hands. You are not stuck. You are deciding, pushed by constraints and blocks and what the world seems to be refusing you, to write your own story as you wish, one more time.

Conclusion for October:

As we are reaching October's completion, you may find it interesting to ask yourself:

- What did you learn about yourself this month?

- Which prompt did you find the most challenging?

- Which prompt was the most enlightening to you, made you discover something about yourself or shifted the way you see things?

- Now that the month is over, and from what you've learned and written, is there a new action you'd like to take to upgrade your life for the best?

"Someone who takes the time to understand their relationship with source, who actively seeks alignment with their broader perspective, who deliberately seeks and finds alignment with who-they-really -are, is more charismatic, more attractive, more effective, and more powerful than a group of millions who have not achieved this alignment."

Esther Hicks

November

November 1

This is a new dawn. What you want is becoming clear. Also, you deserve it. This energy is potent. Divinely orchestrated events are helping you shed an old self. Expect fast and major changes. You are moving into a brand-new reality. You can do this.

November 2

Let me ask you, what's the facet of you, of your unique self and divine spark, that you have not brought out to the greater world enough until now? Write a few lines about this part of you. And here is your commitment for November…Let's embody this more. Let this part of you out. Un-censor yourself. Go! You deserve to fully shine.

____

____

____

____

____

November 3

Allow yourself to reach your deepest spots and waters. You are safe. Today and the next few days most likely won't unfold as you thought. Your own healing process is coming at the forefront. Emotions are coming up to cleanse you. This cleansing is key and you must let it happen. It is realigning your energy with a new grid. You are allowing buried emotions within, and secrets (even old ones) come back to your awareness. This moment is key. Open the door and be free.

____

____

____

____

November 4

Today, write about the idea of leaving. Any thing you left behind you: a marriage, a lover, or a situation. Perhaps it was a job, or an idea about your life. Somebody that passed? Anything. Share a few lines below.

____

____

____

____

November 5

This energy of change is hard to resist. An inner resistance to see the truth is collapsing. It is a point of no return. On the other side of this threshold, you are the Phoenix rising. Put your self-doubt aside. Allow a death to take place. Trust your guts. This is a majestic rebirth.

____

____

____

____

November 6

Let's imagine you are on your deathbed right now. What is the one thing you want to have done, or accomplished, when you reach that moment? If there was one only thing, what would that be?

By the way, I do love this one:

> *"Nobody on their death bed ever worried about their bank balance."*

— Joyce Meyer

____

____

____

____

____

November 7

Something is falling. You have outgrown the limits it was placing on your life. For some, it's been years where you didn't move through such an intense transformation or realization. You must allow pain to keep coming. It's the sign that you are seeing. It's the sign that you are ready to let go. Death always precedes newfound magic.

____

____

____

____

____

November 8

Write about your best sexual experience. Go ahead, and tell me some more! Who were you with? Why was it that good? Why do you think you still recall it today?

November 9

A breakthrough is coming. Your prayers have been heard. Your pain, too. Trust in an order that's bigger than you. Wait a little and take a step back. Stop forcing an outcome or obsessing over it. You need to recharge your soul and allow yourself to receive.

November 10

Tell me today about the moment or day when you felt the most connected to a form of higher power, to the Divine? Perhaps you felt exactly at the right place. Perhaps you felt connected to all that is around. Perhaps you felt guided on your own path. Perhaps you had just experienced a breakthrough. When was that? Write a few lines about this light, precious time below.

November 11

11/11 portal. Fast manifestation gateway. Energy is moving quickly, as if it was unblocked. New ideas are emerging. They are fresh solutions to old issues. You are feeling inspired, ready to go, deeply knowing that you are always eventually finding the right track. The ideas that are emerging right now may be key for the months to come. Listen and flow with the wave.

November 12

Today, let's pick one of your grandparents. Tell them something important. It can be something you already told them, or something you never expressed so far. Write this down below.

November 13

Change is the constant. You can feel this particularly now. You are starting to reassess what is worth of your energy. What gives back as much as you do. What is worth of being developed in time. Who drains and who uplifts. Power, money and love are revaluated in this way. You deserve what's best. You deserve to receive as much as you give.

November 14

Today let me ask you, what is the *one day* when you felt the most proud of yourself? Write some below. When was that? What happened? Bask in this sensation again. You are glorious. You are divine.

November 15

The Eclipse energy is starting to be felt. Movement is happening. Sometimes, you are consciously causing it, sometimes not. The Universe is surprising you. Your prayers are about to be answered in ways that you could have never fathomed. Blessings are coming your way in unpredictable ways. That is what eclipses are all about.

____

____

____

____

____

November 16

If you could go to one place back in time, a place of your past, where would you go? Choose only one! Tell me what that place is below.

____

____

____

____

November 17

Extremely powerful and supportive energy. You have done the work in the past two months. You can take a step back and let it play out. Something that no longer serves is being burned away. On the other side, a new dawn awaits. Let go of control and receive the Universe's help. Magical support from the cosmos surrounds you.

November 18

Courage is a notion that I love. I believe that courage is what allows oneself to take their journey further…truly further. Not to just repeat the same old story, but to actually go beyond. Courage is what enables change. Courage is that inner strength which helps continue in the direction that one feels called to embrace, until it's there. Until it's real. It's what allows humans to keep going even when they can't see. Even especially if the path they are choosing is not the main road, but their own precious, forever in progress, unique line.

Ok so, let's read these five quotes about courage below. What does courage mean to you?

"Courage is not the absence of fear but rather the assessment that something else is more important than fear."

— Franklin D. Roosevelt

"You cannot swim for new horizons until you have courage to lose sight of the shore."

— William Faulkner

"If you are lucky enough to find a way of life you love, you have to find the courage to live it."

— John Irving

"Courage doesn't always roar. Sometimes courage is the little voice at the end of the day that says I'll try again tomorrow."

— Mary Anne Radmacher

"Have the courage to follow your heart and intuition. They somehow already know what you truly want to become. Everything else is secondary."

— Steve Jobs

November 19

Something has been revealed. Anything feels possible. The Universe is with you, trying to get to you in new ways. Let go of the details. Connect with your desires, feel them and let yourself be surprised.

November 20

What do would you truly, utterly, want to see coming to life before the end of the year? What's the one thing you truly want to happen before December 31ˢᵗ?

____

____

____

____

____

November 21

New codes are implementing within you. The Lunar Eclipse caused a massive clearing and now you are re-emerging as the Butterfly. You are growing into a new you that will be fully on board mid-December. Don't overthink change, but follow what inspires now. Your energy is different. You are drawn to doing things another way. Allow this to progressively come to life.

____

____

____

____

November 22

What do you think is holding you back right now? Is there something, someone, or a situation that's keeping you from achieving your goals and dreams?

____

____

____

____

____

November 23

The unknown is calling you. This may feel scary, but Spirit is aligning the right circumstances and people for you to rise into this new timeline. If you feel in the unfamiliar, you are right on time. If you feel inexplicably drawn to situations you didn't even know about a while ago, you are right on time. Celebrate this expansion. You are limitless. You can touch anything new.

____

____

____

____

November 24

What do you think of this quotation? Write a few of your thoughts below.

____

____

____

____

"The secret to happiness is freedom ... and the secret to freedom is courage."

— Thucydides

November 25

You are starting to consciously choose new responses and actions. You are actually doing things differently, which is affecting all around you, reshaping your reality. This took a long time. This year and more. But you can now connect with a deeper layer of your joy, of your soul's purpose. You are co-creating a new timeline so much more aligned with your essence, your soul.

____

____

____

____

November 26

This month, what have you felt that was your most important quality? Tell me about this magical facet of you below!

____

____

____

____

____

November 27

This Eclipse season is not just another cosmic event. It is intense, it is strong. An 18-month karmic window is closing off, freeing you from its lessons. You have learned now. Old limitations and attachments could be just losing their draw. This version of you has never been alive before. Watch around you. Opportunities of a brand new type are about to find you. Keep going. Something is fated and you must continue.

November 28

> *"The secret of life, though, is to fall seven times and to get up eight times."*
>
> — Paulo Coelho, The Alchemist

Is there something you had to try several times before getting it? Something you had to show perseverance about, and not give up, sometimes against all odds, to eventually reach it? What is it?

____

____

____

____

____

November 29

It has been months that you have tried to move the energy in a direction. Success after test - you didn't give up. Sometimes, you kept moving even if everything around you was nebulous, unclear, or even against it. You were stronger than the obstacles. Higher than was what directly in front of you. Keep going. Your path is assured. Your success is under way. All is progressing well. The completion of a phase of patient effort is around the corner. Be proud.

____

____

____

____

____

November 30

I have seen in time, and learned, that our creativity is at our best when we follow our own rhythm. If we are tired, even if we feel pressured by time and deadlines, it's best to rest. This allows the creative juice to come back stronger, more sparkly, and to actually respect our deadlines with more ease! If we feel that we are in a creative flow, it's often a good advice to make the most of it, allow inspiration to flow through us without restriction.

Do you agree with this? Have you noticed this creative rhythm in your own life? Can you trust it? Do you trust that if you are not that creative this week, and need rest or to do something else, you'll most likely be vibrantly creative again in a couple of weeks or so?

If you are a woman, have you noticed any connection between your creative cycle and your Moon, or menstrual, cycle? Tell me your thoughts!

____

____

____

____

____

Conclusion for November:

As we are reaching November's completion, you may find it interesting to ask yourself:

- What did you learn about yourself this month?

- Which prompt did you find the most challenging?

- Which prompt was the most enlightening to you, made you discover something about yourself or shifted the way you see things?

- Now that the month is over, and from what you've learned and written, is there a new action you'd like to take to upgrade your life for the best?

"I knew that if I allowed fear to overtake me, my journey was doomed. Fear, to a great extent, is born of a story we tell ourselves, and so I chose to tell myself a different story from the one women are told. I decided I was safe. I was strong."

Cheryl Strayed

December

December 1

At this point, something is no longer under your control. The Eclipse is working like a fated storm of light in your life. You must let go. Take one day, one moment at a time. Your wishes are about to be granted, as if your dreams were at last hatching out from the ground after months of back and forth. Inside of you, you feel strange but clear. You know what is good for you. What is soul truth. Keep going. The elevation into a new timeline will reach its peak on December 4th.

____

____

____

____

____

December 2

Hello, fellow wanderer! Tell me, who are you? A "gardener" or a "builder"? Read below!

> *Hello, fellow wanderer! Tell me, who are you? A "planter" or a "builder"? Paulo Coelho teaches that we can adopt the attitude of the builder, or the attitude of the planter. Builders take as much time as needed to finish tasks—but they finish. They are illuminated when building, and diminished when the building stops. For planters, their work is also never done. The garden is a place to plant, build, grow and change over time.*
>
> — Paulo Coelho

____

____

____

____

December 3

You prayed your way out of something. Your way out is about to come. Expect major blessing and miracles in the next few weeks. A significant layer of karma has been released. Believe in yourself. Believe in your gifts. The universe is bringing you the unexpected, all for your highest good.

December 4

Who has been your most important teacher up until now? By teacher, I mean at an academic level, or spiritual one, or through a course you took... anything! Who is the teacher that left the biggest imprint on you?

December 5

This is an intense window, with many of us still clearing deep layers. There is a need for rest, self-care and self-compassion. Fear could be involved, as well as feeling that many paths are available or could represent the new. The dust hasn't settled, yet. This Eclipse season was super potent. Allow everything to percolate, to implement. You will know, you will feel, when it is time for more inspired action.

December 6

What's the creative thing that you did that you are the most proud of?

December 7

Your confidence is being restored. Today and tomorrow, you are receiving important messages, words and wisdom of truth. Something is starting to find an ease. A rhythm. Life is not a race. Small steps are enough. You have moved so much energy within to get there. Congratulate yourself. You are immensely supported.

December 8

What is the one thing you'd like to say to your mother today? It can be something you already expressed to her, or never did! Go ahead and tell me about it below.

December 9

Please never allow anyone to tell you that you are hard to love. Please believe in yourself. Please trust someone will *get* you. You are not hard to love. You have wounds, like we all do, and you have needs. And somewhere, somewhere in this stormy world, someone will get you. Be there for you. Love you as you are.

December 10

What is the one thing you'd like to say to your father today? It can be something you already expressed to him, or never did! Go ahead and tell me about it below.

____

____

____

____

____

December 11

Large influx of positive and high energy, already present or about to come. What's not meant to stay is being washed away. You are practicing giving yourself joy and that is the secret. Don't hustle, but align. Don't exhaust yourself but practice the wisdom of divine timing and divine moments for rest and integration. Soul is leading the way, making you feel drawn to certain things and further away from others. Trust the process.

____

____

____

____

December 12

What is the moment of your life you felt the most resilient? Share about this below.

December 13

To thrive in this energy, you have to stay on your lane and let other souls' dramas, difficulties and mutual triggers outside of your golden shield of protection as much as possible. So much is happening both on individual and collective levels. You are staying on the path that's calling you and trying to not be that distracted by the processes happening around you. This path, you have never walked it before in that way. That is why you need all your inner bravery and trust in a Higher Power to keep elevating, without apologies.

December 14

I love the word "hero." It is powerful, and it has many meanings. For some, being a hero is connected with the act of being perseverant. For others, it's about being on a mission that's greater than their own selves. For others, it's about what one endured, and how they have overcome obstacles and difficulties. Let's read the quotations below. What does hero or heroine mean to you?

"I like it when a flower or a little tuft of grass grows through a crack in the concrete. It's so fuckin' heroic."

— George Carlin

Heroes were ordinary people who knew that even if their own lives were impossibly knotted, they could untangle someone else's. And maybe that one act could lead someone to rescue you right back."

— Jodi Picoult

"Living by faith includes the call to something greater than cowardly self-preservation."

— J.R.R. Tolkien

"Hard times don't create heroes. It is during the hard times that the "hero" within us is revealed."

— Bob Riley

December 15

Big rebirth energy. The old is leaving your body and mind fast, having less and less power over you. The Feminine principle within yourself is experiencing a major cleansing, which will help it lead the way and guide you more and more in the next few days. Expect aha moments and epiphanies. Deep down, you know what must get your attention now. Deep down, you are finding yourself again, in a new form, as if from a higher point of view. Your energy is finding an ease, a coming back to the Self, one more time.

December 16

We are almost at the end of the year, and therefore of this book! How has writing helped you? What do you think of writing as a way of self-discovery? Have these prompts helped you find something about yourself, or relearn something?

December 17

The energy has already shifted to another timeline. Even to other goals. Many moments and the unfolding of the year have led you to this point where the story changes. Right now, it's hard to see clearly. It's foggy. It could feel heavy, too. Your greatest power is found in trusting a Higher Power to lead your feet. You can't see it all, but you are still walking the story of your greatness. One step at a time, through faith and gentle moves. You are exactly where you are supposed to be.

____

____

____

____

December 18

Do you agree with this?

"Silence is a cage. These words are my wings."

— Jenim Dibie

Let's keep reflecting on this writing experience that you've had through this book. Was it healing for you? How did it help?

____

____

____

____

December 19

Major time of transformation. We can already feel this next year will be of a different energy with rewards of a different kind. Things are not going to be the same. Magic is happening behind the scenes in order to match this new version of you. You are being elevated into your next phase. The process is accelerating. Let go and be moved.

____

____

____

____

December 20

Amongst the several areas of your life (career, love, friends, family, creativity, pets…) which one do you feel has grown the most this year? Share an anecdote which illustrates this below!

____

____

____

____

December 21

This the lead to the last Full Moon of the year. You are leaving behind what isn't coming with you in for the next year. You are starting to feel more confident in your own skin. A major layer of self-doubt is being let go of. You deserve the best. Trust what inspires you. Feel your vision. You have the power to make it real. You are manifesting your future now.

December 22

Christmas is coming! We all have something that we like about this time of the year. Share below, what are your favorite pieces of this time of the year? That could even be one detail of the Christmas celebration in your home!

December 23

This year has been overwhelming at times. You have made it. Flown through the highs and lows. The constant realizations, tests and shifts. Congratulate yourself for not giving up on the way. Now the plan will keep unfolding. Be open. New possibilities are coming your way. You are finding more possibilities for your gifts to bloom. Make space to receive this renewal.

December 24

Interesting question today…what do you think are the most important qualities for you in a lover?

December 25

An energy that's new, or maybe that you weren't expecting, is starting to lead you. Life doesn't often, in truth, respect our mind's plan. Let yourself go in that new direction. Explore. Open up. Let things be as you are feeling now. Let the flow of your evolution be what it is. You are ok. You are safe. You are opening the door of a new room - feeling so amazed and joyful to be there. Trust the magic of life. You wouldn't feel that way if it wasn't time.

____

____

December 26

"Joy. Don't seek something, or someone, but seek Joy — as a feeling within, as a vibration inside, as an energy."

— Sophie Gregoire, "She is the Moon"

Meditate on this one. Do you agree? To what extent is joy something that can come from within?

____

____

____

____

____

December 27

Old foundations and ways you thought about things would be are collapsing. This is for your highest good. You must be brave enough to change the story, to own your truth so much that it becomes more important than what you could lose by embodying it. You are in the in-between. Trust yourself. External circumstances are realigning to match you. You are constantly guided and soon you will see that your desires were greatly supported by the force of life, too.

____

____

____

____

____

December 28

Alright, this wonderful year is reaching completion. You have good times. Great ones, even. You also experienced setbacks, lower times, blocks on your road. Go ahead and tell me below your most favorite, precious moments of the year!

____

____

____

____

____

____

December 29

Your inner world is changing. Old patterns are falling and you may feel in the unknown - in a strange space within, and with others. This shift is unstoppable. Remember that you have the power. In fact you always have the power to choose to evolve. You are strong enough to be there, in this energy. Have faith. This is all for your highest good.

____

____

____

____

____

December 30

This is the end of our journey together, at least for now. There will be others, this I'm sure! 😊 List below the two or three things you have loved, or you have learned, about life, or yourself, through this book's journey!

____

____

____

____

December 31

This time feels like a void but it isn't energetically. You are feeling what must grow and what is dissolving. You are starting to make plans for the following year because the truth of your heart is becoming clearer. You are regaining strength and clarity, and this will lead you to key places for your path. Regroup before it starts. This time is highly valuable.

____

____

____

____

Bonus prompt!

- Think back to a year from now. What has changed? What has remained the same?

- What was the overall theme of this year?

- And, what do you want the next for next year to be?

Conclusion for December:

As we are reaching December's completion, you may find it interesting to ask yourself:

- What did you learn about yourself this month?

- Which prompt did you find the most challenging?

- Which prompt was the most enlightening to you, made you discover something about yourself or shifted the way you see things?

- Now that the month is over, and from what you've learned and written, is there a new action you'd like to take to upgrade your life for the best?

"The most important kind of freedom is to be who you really are. (...) There can't be any large scale revolution until there is a personal revolution, on an individual level. It's got to happen inside first."

Jim Morrison

Extra - A Tale for the New Year

Your fire is never lost.

Nobody - and nothing - can extinguish, annihilate, destroy who you are.

You are always on the verge of being back.

Back to who your soul is.

Back to yourself, fully powerful - fully lit up.

You are always one moment, one step away from your full come back to soul's spirit, magic and gold.

They will never stop you. You will never be made small.

You are never being placed in a corner.

You are the sacred fire made flesh & blood.

You are always, if not already, one step from being fully back.

May you feel your inner fire fully on.

May they all feel your power.

May you never dim your light. May you never dim your light.

Conclusion

Yay! You have done it, mission completed on your end!

What's the message here? Remember to take time for yourself daily. Remember to always be willing to take a deeper dive within. There is always more to learn about ourselves. We are a work in progress. We can always access more information about who we are. And it's not always necessary to go to the other side of the world or do something crazy to reveal more about ourselves. See, a notebook and pen, it works as well!

Blessings on your journey, Fellow Wanderer.

Acknowledgements

Thank you to the several authors who joyfully endorsed this work and shared their beautiful words of encouragement. Thank you for this, but also for your support all the way though the realization of my writer's dreams.

Many thanks to Pauline Bernadet, very talented French photographer, for her many beautiful shots taken in the very favorite green spot of my hometown (www.paulinebernadet.com). How gifted you are! Any soul will be shining through your work.

A big thank you and hug to Becky Hernandez, who has been my guide, teacher and ethereal cheerleader over the years. We are always connected. May your walking feet be blessed by the light! (www.misfityogi.com)

Many thanks to Nelly Pierre-Justin, graphic designer, for such an adapted, highly intuitive and talented contribution to the cover design - and so many thanks for your advice in other aspects of the projects!

And of course many thanks to Tiffany Harelik, awesome publisher, who showed the patience and professional skills that I needed to complete this work. Thank you for finding me at the most perfect time!

And even if you still can't read, a big warm thanks to my baby boy Mikado, white big cat, for following me through all the projects I have had over the years since 2014 - including several geographic moves that you gracefully joined (even in Asia!), many papers and articles that I wrote at the weirdest hours of the day (or night), and always your warm, calm, soothing but energetic presence in my life. Thank you for always bringing me back to the light. What a team of felines we are!

A big, magical hug to the awesome artist Heather Reynolds (@ dream_life_studios) for all your powerful art that you generously share with the world - and for creating such a cosmically aligned canvas of the white cat.

About the author

Sophie Gregoire is a transformation coach, author, hypnotherapist, astrologer, and specialist in multigenerational healing, prenatal and birth trauma healing. She left much of her life at the age of 29 and took her chance to explore herself through years of inner work and personal development, and worldwide solo travels. Sophie's passion is to help other tap into their highest potential and embody their most fulfilled and empowered selves in the world.

Sophie works with people internationally and locally in Toulouse. She has been featured in several personal development online magazines and developed her own community and readership on social medias. She published her first book, *"She is the Moon"*, in 2019, and will publish her first short stories collection in 2023". Sophie gives online creative and therapeutic writing classes and hosts Women Circles locally. She lives with her partner in her French pink-city, Toulouse. Her greatest muse and favorite life-companion is her traveler cat, Mikado.

Find more about Sophie here:

www.sophiegregoire.com

www.sophiegregoirehypnotherapeute.com

@sophiegregoires

Sophie also created the foundation Rainbow Pets, to support families moving through the passing of their beloved animal (www.rainbowpets.fr).

Also from Sophie Gregoire:

"She is the Moon: A Journey of Self-Discovery",

published in 2019 with Golden Dragonfly Press.

9 7 9 8 9 8 5 3 5 2 3 2 0

About the Author

Aga Arvind, a Post graduate in Law is a 52-year-old corporate Lawyer. Her under graduation is in English Literature from the prestigious Maharajas College, Ernakulam. She had practiced law over a decade, before the Hon'ble High court at Madras and later shifted to inhouse roles of Corporates.

This is a debut venture of the author into the literary world. This Novel is a gentle attempt to portray the dilemma of a girl of mixed ethnicity, as well as challenges of a patriarchal family woven together with unconditioned love to each other.

Aga is married to Arvind, who is a Mechanical Engineer working for a reputed Oil and Gas enterprise in Middle East. Their only daughter is Deepshika, an IITian and a voracious reader from her young age.

Aga's parents live in a quaint village nearby Kalady town, which is renowned to be known for the birth place of Jagatguru Sri Adi Shankaracharya* (An Indian Vedic scholar, philosopher and teacher of Advaita Vedanta, who lived approximately during the period of 788 AD- 800 AD).

Her father, K.N Bhaskaran is a retired class one officer and mother a retired High school teacher. The love for literature was inculcated in Aga right from her child hood by her parents. Those where the days of English comics like Tinkle, Amarchithrakathas and there were other comics in Malayalam, (the vernacular language), like Poombatta. Balarema, Ambili ammavan etc to name a few. These books were Aga's constant companions before she could lay hands on to hard core literature works.

The habit of reading English Daily 'The Hindu' and the weeklies, the fortnightlies and the monthlies (which was bought by her father), like Reader's Digest, The Illustrated weekly of India in which R K Laxman's and Mario Miranda's Cartoons featured, instilled the early love for English language in Aga. Those days Aga had her father's surname and was known as Aga Bhaskar. Her only brother Agesh Bhaskar's eleven-year-old son Aagney Agesh is an author of two books.

Contents

Chapter 1

Money Order From England

10ᵗʰ June 1978, Cochin

"Post," the postman loudly announced his arrival along with his cycle bell, "triinnggg."

75-year-old Raghavan looked up from the "Malayala Manorama" daily newspaper which he was reading and with his usual Cochin slang, asked, "Ente makante letter unda?"

Every month, he waits for it; his son works as a translator in England, in the English courts, where illegal immigrants are tried. He sends money through some postal mechanism from England so his septuagenarian father gets it at his doorstep.

Raghavan's eldest son, Bhaskaran's payday is the 30ᵗʰ of every month, and precisely after 10 days, the postman arrives with a letter and money order in Cochin.

Postman sat on the verandah and took off the crossly hung withered leather bag from his shoulders, and carefully opened it. A lot of currency notes of different denominations that are rolled and tied neatly with rubber bands were seen in the bag. He took a roll from it and kept his thick-framed spectacles on the nose when he looked like an Extraterritorial with bulged eyeballs with those lenses magnifying his eyeballs for the onlooker. He skimmed through the small piece of paper wrapped around it; it read some other recipient's name. He kept it back carefully and took out another one. This time, it was the right one, so he carefully started counting it. Raghavan noticed that the postman was sweating profusely, and his uniform was entirely drenched. The summer had already been taken over by rain, and this day, there were signs of rain, too. The clouds had started darkening, but the atmosphere was deeply humid.

Raghavan slightly turned his neck towards the kitchen and called out, "Saro, postman vannittundu enthengilum kudikkaan kodu." **

There was a female voice from the kitchen acknowledging it. The Mangalore tile-roofed house, might be as old as Raghavan himself, had a small verandah and 2 rooms along with a kitchen. There was a big kanikonna (golden shower) tree in the front yard, which sheds yellow flowers during the summer season. These flowers are used for Vishu Kani ***, and neighbours also come to pluck these flowers for their homes too. As it was already June and the rains had started pouring, the blooms were all withered and gone. A sparrow's nest as well as a weaver bird's nest were seen hanging on the branches. There was a wooden birdhouse fixed by his youngest son Krishnan, who is a sailor, on the side walls of the house, where some pigeons had made their nesting home. The pigeons happily sat on the sills of the windows and dirtied them with their droppings at their wish. At times, these pigeons were seen coyishly to their mate. There was a decoy nest of a crow too on the golden shower tree, where a Koel was seen trying to sneak in to lay her eggs. The Koel desperately left the decoy nest as it found that the nest was not occupied. It flew away in search of a nest with eggs laid, to get her offspring to be raised freely by a crow.

When Raghavan's younger sons, Thangavel and Krishnan, got married, 2 more rooms, which were just like a shack, were added at the backyard of the house to accommodate their families.

Meanwhile, his elder son Bhaskaran, who was in London, and his second son Divakaran, who worked in Bhutan, shared the costs and bought a terrace house next door. Thus, the acquired extra space was juggled between 4 families and their children. Raghavan's 3 daughters, Radha, Renuka, and Rema, were all married and lived in nearby towns.

Suddenly, an old lady's frail voice from one of the inner rooms was heard, "Aaa ezhuthangaadu vayiche." ****

Raghavan, in an angry tone, replied that they should wait and be patient as the letter is yet to be opened. The postman finished counting the currencies and mentioned that this time there are a few coins as the British pound has gained a bit more than last month.

Meanwhile, a lady in her early thirties, must be Saro who was beckoned by Raghavan, came out with a steel tumbler full of 'sambharam' (butter milk mixed with ginger, curry leaves, and salt). She kept mixing it with a small wooden spatula with its scoop up.

Sarojaya was a fair, plump lady. She was wearing a cotton saree with the 'pallu' (various saree tying methods) tucked into the other side of her hip, showing that she was busy in the kitchen.

She looked into the currency notes covetously and silently handed over the cup of buttermilk to the postman. The postman drank the cool buttermilk with such relish, in one single gasp, and with a big sigh of relief smiled at her. Sarojaya took back the steel mug from him and went inside the kitchen; she was indeed in a hurry as it was about to be 12 o'clock and the old lady would now start shouting for lunch.

The postman could hear the old woman's voice saying, "Saro Saro choraaya," ***** but could not hear any reply to that.

Raghavan exclaimed that Saro has only 2 hands, and he turned to the postman and told him that Saro, his third daughter-in-law, is struggling alone in the kitchen from early morning.

"Cheval koovumbo eneettu ithu thane." ******

The postman nodded, seconding him, while wiping his face with a soiled kerchief that he had pulled out from his shirt's collar. He gave a bunch of papers on which he had marked a cross symbol with his pencil for Raghavan to sign. Raghavan, who was ready with his hero company's ink pen, signed his name neatly in English.

Raghavan was the driver of an Englishman who owned a hotel in Fort Cochin during the 1930s. Later, he handed over the business to Settu (a local ****Kachi community businessman) and left for England. Raghavan learnt the English alphabet from his ex-boss's children during his free time.

Robert Bristow had started working at Cochin port as the chief engineer in 1921 under the direction of Lord Wellington, the then governor of Madras, and he completed the work in a span of 21 years. The hotel of Raghavan's employer thrived with business during this time, as many English engineers' families frequently visited Cochin. Most of them had settled in Madras, which was around 500 miles away from Kochi, as it was much more modern and suited their lifestyle. They all had vacation bungalows in the hills to survive the peak summer season too.

Raghavan continued as Sett's driver, as the Englishman had sold his big, long Plymouth car to Sett for 10,000 rupees (Indian Rupee) in 1945. The sayippu ********* had full of praises for his chauffeur too; he gifted a Swiss made wristwatch to Raghavan as a ticking token of love, in sayyippu's own words. Later, Raghavan's son during one of his visits from London had told Raghavan, the watch named Rolex would have been worth 50 pounds in those days, i.e. equivalent to approximately 500 rupees. Raghavan could have bought the rented house he was staying in his own name for that much money in those days. He could not think about selling his Rolex watch gifted by his master, even though he did not own a piece of land in his own name. Now his second son, Divakaran, who is running an antique shop in Jew Street, says that Rolex, which is a rotary type, is very much sought after by the watch company itself, and they will indeed buy it back for a huge price if it is found to be their original make. Money never lured Raghavan to temptations; he was a contented person, hence did not bother to know about the price that it might fetch.

The postman completed his duty, tucked back his soiled kerchief into his shirt's collar, and waved at Raghavan before he mounted his bicycle. Raghavan now started counting the currencies. After counting, he got up to enter his room. Before stepping into the room, he removed his Bata slippers and placed them outside the verandah. His room was the best room in the house, with a neat red oxide-laid, daily swabbed floor, a rosewood single cot with a cotton mattress neatly covered with 'Co-Optex' bedsheets. In one corner stood a teakwood Almirah, the only piece of furniture. This Almirah was the only 'Streedhan' (gift from the bride's family) brought by Dakshayani during their marriage. Dakshayani has her version of a detailed story about the Almirah, made by local artisans in her village; it was her father's specially curated gift for his only daughter. The wall of Raghavan's room displayed a black & white photo of his wife Dakshayani and himself; one could not guess their age from the photo. The corner of the photo bore Krishnan Nair Studio's rubberstamp impression. Raghavan's face in the photograph resembled that of his elder son Bhaskaran, who is now in his mid-forties. Hence, it can be presumed that the photograph was taken when Raghavan too was in his mid-forties. Another photograph showed Raghavan in his chauffeur's uniform, taken just a week before his retirement, also hung on the wall.

He took out a bunch of keys from his hip belt pocket and opened the wooden Almirah, where he had kept all his personal belongings. The topmost shelf had a secret box hidden behind a small cabinet, which from the outside looked like a plank. He opened the cabinet by sliding the plank to the side and took out another wooden box. He carefully placed the box on his cot and took a small key from his bunch to open it. The box was opened widely, and he cautiously placed the wad of rolled notes in it, locked it again, and kept it back safely. He took a hardbound blue notebook from the almirah and a pencil from the tray, where a few more pens, pencils, and a Chepauk blue ink bottle were kept. Next to the tray was a small mud piggy bank where the loose coins, out of the remaining money after expenses, were put. When Vishu comes, he will break it, count the coins, and divide them into equal parts to give to his grandchildren as Vishu kaineettam **********. In the next 2 racks, his white dhotis and white shirts were neatly ironed and kept. In between the clothes, the wrappers of 'Camay' soaps were placed so that the fragrance lingered mildly on his clothes.

The bottom-most rack held some biscuit tins named Danish biscuits, now filled with locally available cookies from the English bakery down Jewish Synagogue Street (he will refill a small glass jar kept in the meal safe in the dining room as it is Angelina's tea time snack) and a few photo albums consisting of family events photographed. In a small handwoven basket were a few 'Camay' and 'Chandrika' soaps. Camay soaps were brought by Bhaskaran from England and Chandrika soaps by Raghavan himself from 'Motilal's kada*' (local name for the merchant's shop). He will give his wife Dakshayani one Chandrika soap for the whole month and shall not give an additional one, even if their grandchildren use it and finish it off. The children use it by whisking it without her knowledge. Raghavan was a disciplined man, as seen even from his well-arranged Almirah. At times when their daughters visit, Dakshayani gets money from them and struggles on her own to the nearby shop to make her own small purchases too. Her second daughter Renuka was married to a rich merchant who had a wholesale of spices; hence she was the one who frequently gave lavish amounts as pocket money to Dakshayani. The old lady had elephantiasis and found it very difficult to move around with her heavy limbs. She had a small trunk box under her cot, and a small key was kept under her pillow. She counts her money every day to ensure that none has tried to swindle it. On one such occasion, she read in the newspaper that gold had touched 500 Rs per sovereign. She got an idea and set off to the goldsmith's shop; this clever woman started buying small coins with whatever money she collected from her daughters.

Raghavan came back to his armchair on the verandah and opened the book. The hardbound blue notebook was full of sums, additions, and subtractions. The crumpled pages with faded ink denote that the book was quite old. He carefully turned the pages to find an unwritten page. It seems that only a few more pages are left in the book. He took out the 'hero pen' which he had tucked

in his pocket after signing the money order, wrote "Om" *****
towards the centre at the top of the page, and then to the right
side of the page, he wrote 10-6-1978.

Just one line below that, he wrote – Ru 1015 (in Malayalam
which denotes Rupee).

This is the amount with which he needs to run the expenses
of a family of 4 adults and 4 children.

Thangavel, his third son, and wife Sarojaya, along with
their 3 children, Romila, Raju, and Roma, lived with Raghavan
and his wife. Thangavel, who is in his mid-thirties, was a
trained electrician but too lazy to take up any job. He knew his
elder brother is sending their father a good amount monthly,
sufficient to run the family. He had rich friends in the city and
he too, like them, always wore a Terylene shirt and bell-bottom
pants, smearing good Athar (perfume). The Athar too was a gift
from his youngest brother Krishnan, who is a sailor. He bought
it from Mumbai as a gift for his brother when he visited them
during one of his vacations. Krishnan had the habit of buying
foreign goods from the Bombay markets and lavishly giving gifts
to all the family members.

The fourth child mentioned in the family is Angelina, the
daughter of Bhaskaran, who lives in London now, and he is the
one sending a monthly allowance to Raghavan without fail.

Raghavan continued writing in his notebook, Angie (as she
was addressed by him), in Malayalam, and he started listing

1)   School fees – 20 Rupees
2)   Tuition fees for Missy – 10 Rupees
3)   Horlicks/biscuits – 5 Rupees

4)   Pocket money – 2 Rupees
5)   Cycle rickshaw Wala rent – 5 Rupees
6)   Ration shop – 88 Rupees
7)   Palacharakku (Stationery shop) – 275 Rupees
8)   Paal(Milk) – 50 Rupees
9)   School thorappu* (opening*) uniform books – 120 Rupees
10) Tailor – 30 Rupees
11) Dakshayani Ayurveda marunnu (medicine) – 17 Rupees
12) Newspaper – 3 Rupees
13) Meen (fish) – 60 Rupees

(Total: 648 Rupees)

He tucked the pen back into his shirt pocket and started rechecking his addition carefully, with his pencil pointed towards each item. Before he could complete it, Sarojaya (called "Saro") appeared at the front door and announced that lunch was ready.

He looked at the pendulum clock kept on the verandah and saw it was precisely 1 o'clock and again looked at his wristwatch too. That was a habit of years, which he always does as soon as he completes his morning bath. His face glowed with happiness and he exclaimed for no reason that the time on the wall clock and wristwatch matched. Maybe small reasons bring a smile to people's otherwise stressed-out faces. Raghavan got up slowly from his chair, wore his slippers, and held onto the door frame to enter the dining room of the house, which was one step higher than the front verandah. The cat which was lying down in the verandah suddenly ran along with Raghavan to the dining room; it brushed against Raghavan's legs and ran outside the passage meowing. The dining table was just a desk placed towards the corner of the passage, near a small window with a faded curtain, and the table was covered with a floral-printed plastic table cover. It was purchased from the vendor who brings small knick-knack household items on his bicycle carrier. A few homemade pickles were also kept on the side of the table in small 'Bharani' (urns used in Indian kitchens).

Raghavan's lunch spread had 'kuthari choru'* (brown rice*) on a slightly pitted white porcelain plate and a smaller side plate with the same pattern, on which his special 'meen'* (fish*) curry was served.

Raghavan's daily morning chores include going to the local fish market to fetch fresh catches. He will buy a slightly costly fish named kingfish or mullet in a very small quantity for himself and other cheaper varieties of fish, namely mackerel, sardines, or small prawns for the rest of the family from a specific fisherwoman named Mariamma. Mariamma's husband is an angler, which gives her an edge over other vendors in the market. He even has a monthly account book with this fish vendor, which she enters daily and he pays correctly every month (he sticks to his budget of 60 rupees in total every month). After all, he is the patriarchal head of the family and he deserves to be treated well; hence, the costly fish dish is considered his privilege in the family.

Sarojaya manages to give a portion of 'special meen* (fish*) curry' to Thangavel too, by further cutting down the pieces into smaller ones, so that the old man will not realise this adjustment, if the same number of pieces bought by him are served to him. Her husband is her god incarnation and she just adores him and at times proudly claims that 'Thangan chettan' (wives usually address their husbands by adding chettan to their names in the Cochin area), resembles 'Prem Nazir', a famous Malayalam film star of those times. But nobody else except her has thought or felt the same.

There was one more dish called 'thoran'* (boiled vegetable*, usually spring beans, or carrots, or beetroots, or raw bananas, etc., garnished in coconut oil, with mustards, fenugreek, green chilies, and grated coconut). Today, this 'thoran' was made out of finely chopped raw bananas and was served in another quarter plate to complete Raghavan's lunch spread.

One small bowl of ordinary white rice (this is bought from the civil supplies shop – called ration shop, which was given on subsidised rates by the Government) was also kept near this. Cats as well as others in the house except Raghavan and Anjelina eat the same ration rice. He murmured a small gratitude prayer and took 2 to 3 grains of rice and kept them aside on the quarter plate, in which vegetable 'thoran' was kept. He finished eating everything except the 3 grains of rice that were kept aside. He then poured the leftover fish curry into the bowl of white rice and walked towards the bucket of water kept outside the passage to wash his hands. He emptied the rice from the bowl into an old worn-out aluminium plate and kept the bowl aside. Raghavan now took the plastic mug which was tied to a rope that hung from the wooden ceiling, long enough to dip it into the bucket of water, and washed his hands and mouth thoroughly. Then he reached for a small soap box with soggy green 'Chandrika' soap pieces in it and rinsed again to ward off the fish smell from his hands. He then poured water into another plastic bowl kept near the bucket, where the cat was patiently waiting for him; it just brushed onto his legs with gratitude before it started eating.

He came back to his room after lunch and looked at his watch, and thought today he must wait for Bhaskaran's monthly call at Divakaran's house around 4 pm after his evening tea, and slipped into his normal routine of an afternoon nap. The cat too had followed him back to his room, sneaking under his cot, licking its paws, and slipping into its usual nap too.

English Translations of Malayalam transliterations used in the above chapter

*What is it? My son's letter!

**Read aloud that letter.

***right from the rooster's calls in the morning

****The Kutch Muslim community in Fort Cochin consists of traders who migrated to Fort Cochin from Gujarat.

***** Vishu, Vishu Kani, and Vishu Kaineettam are part of Vishu, a local festival in Kerala. It is considered an auspicious day for starting cultivating activities in rural Kerala.

******Vishu Kani – The first sight of viewing God adorned in jewels along with food grains, as well as vegetables.

*******Vishukaineettam – the oldest member of the family gifts coins after viewing Vishukani.

* * *

Chapter 2

Bhaskaran's New Family

England, events from 30th May 1978 to 10th June 1978

Bhaskaran collected his pay cheque from the Administration office and searched for his reporting officer. He found him at the lunch table. Bhaskaran knocked on the glass pane outside the verandah and gestured with his thumbs up.

Mr Smith, his boss too gestured back with a nod of approval. Every month Bhas, as addressed by his fellow colleagues, ensures that he deposits 100 British pounds in the head post office to wire transfer to India to his father and a small amount to his brother who co-owned his house in Cochin, as the very first thing as soon as he receives his pay check. He had promised his father that he will, without fail, send the amount required for household expenses, while he had left his 3-year-old girl under his father's care in India in the year 1970. Bhaskaran is a man of his word, rain or shine or the day hit with the worst snowfall, he goes to the head post office every month by changing 2 tube trains and a bus, taking special permission from the court officer, Mr Smith, whom he reports to. It takes half an hour to get to the post office and another half an hour to complete the formal requirements in the PO. Every month Bhasi skips his lunch on payday and makes use of the one-hour recess and takes an additional half an hour permission time.

Due to this recurring activity, he had befriended a clerk in the PO who always completed the process quite quickly. The clerk handed over the 2 wire transfer receipts in a Royal Mail envelope.

Bhaskaran could return to his workplace without too much delay.

There might be 2 or 3 trials going on in the County court where he must translate Malayalam, Tamil, or Hindi according to the nativity of the Indian or Tamil-speaking Sri Lankans. These people are tried for petty offences like theft of a small amount from the wayside shops, shoplifting, or being involved in a drunken brawl or any other torts. They are unable to utter a proper sentence in English; hence, a translator is required. Only once in the last decade of his work, Bhas was asked to assist the court in understanding the original situation of a Hindi-speaking Indian origin lady who brutally assaulted her twice-aged, British-origin drunkard husband. The stories were all pathetic, and the court too felt sympathetic at certain situations, all because of Bhasi's language skills. The court will take steps on humanitarian grounds in such cases. Bhasi had left Kerala after his matriculation and had spent his young age in the Bombay Presidency. During those days, he was working in a logistics company that had its Headquarters in the Madras Presidency. Thus, he had to frequent the warehouses spread across the Madras Presidency too. This hands-on experience made him an expert in both Hindi and Tamil languages.

The day was a bit cloudy, so the rains, which were just ready to pour, started off with a bit of a storm. A huge lash of wind swept along the dry leaves on the roads, making them sway up and down, resembling brown butterflies.

All pedestrians suddenly took shelter under the portico of the Post Office. A few of them just paused long enough to take out umbrellas from their bags and opened them to continue their walk. Due to the strong winds, they too had to come back running. Others who had raincoats in their bags took them out, wore them, and continued walking.

"Oh no," Bhasi thought. He will miss the trial that might start in another half an hour, and buses were all getting filled up before he could get in.

Suddenly, the rain stopped as if the universe listened to his inner whisper, and pedestrians who had decided to jump into the bus changed their decision and continued to walk.

Another bus stopped in front of the PO, and he returned just 2 minutes before the court resumed. Bhasi whispered a silent gratitude prayer.

The court officer called out the names of the accused, and Bhasi repeated the counsel's questions in Tamil to the accused and started keenly listening to the answers. He quickly translated the Tamil words to English, which were taken down in shorthand by the stenographer. Mrs. Margaret Williams, the stenographer, will type it the next day and take Bhasi's signature before the judge sees the file again.

Bhasi is not comfortable calling Margaret 'Maggie' like other colleagues did; he alone addressed her as Mrs. Williams. At first, Margaret thought it was normal, as it was always the British way of showing respect. Later, she learnt from others that Margaret was the name of Bhasi's estranged ex-wife. Bhasi was married to an English lady in 1965 and had 2 children: one stepson from Margaret's first marriage and one daughter born to him.

When both decided to part ways, his wife wanted the custody of their daughter. The stepson's name was James and the younger one a girl named Angelina. When the fights over children recurred quite often, Margaret tutored James not to go out alone with his stepfather as he would take him away from his mother. The little girl couldn't understand any of this, and one day she was taken out by Bhas to travel another 20 hours and reached Kochi. From then on, he had to face a lot of lawsuits in England. Their respective attorneys advised both to mutually agree to divorce and put a full stop to the claims and counterclaims. They agreed, and a formal court order decided that the custody of the daughter shall be with Bhasi as agreed. The little girl, Anjie, was completely entrusted to her father to be brought up as an Indian girl.

Time passed, and court was dismissed for the day. Bhasi neatly arranged the desk, signed the ledger, and left the courtroom for the locker room. He took a small key from his pouch and opened locker number 5 to retrieve his bag. After taking out the deodorant bottle and spraying a bit to freshen up, he returned it to the locker. Inside, there was a medicine box with a Red Cross sign on it. He took out a "Strepsils" tablet and placed it in his mouth. He then securely stored some files related to his office work in the locker, double-checking the handle to ensure it was locked. Bhasi placed the bunch of keys back into his hand purse pouch, which could barely hold the keys and looked bulgy as it also accommodated a few pennies.

He then moved to the coat stand and, after taking out his long coat and a hat that were kept together, he wore his long coat. He looked into the mirror to adjust the collar and placed the hat onto his head to hide his baldness.

He grabbed his umbrella without much searching, which was kept in an umbrella holder along with other umbrellas next to the coat stand. His umbrella had a special wooden handle that resembled a pig (in actuality, it was supposed to be an elephant head) which he crafted himself for uniqueness. The story of the umbrella handle goes like this: each time someone would take home other people's umbrellas mistakenly, as almost all handles were the curvy wooden type.

Bhas had designed his own umbrella handle and tried to sculpt an elephant head. But due to his amateur skills, he inadvertently chopped off the long trunk, and it turned out to look like a pig's nose, thus becoming a pig's head. His colleagues in court remembered the old currency where George IV was wearing a chain with an elephant head locket, and it resembled as if he was wearing a pig locket on the currency. This, in turn, offended the Muslim citizens of the country, and the currency had to be withdrawn by His Majesty.

Then onwards Bhas's umbrella was called a piggy head. He stepped out of the court complex and headed towards the bus station. He greeted the driver and collected his tickets from the vending machine before sitting in his usual seat. He sat and looked at the court complex, uttering his usual gratitude prayer. The court complex was painted with dull white paint and looked as if ash was smothered over it. The unpruned willow trees covered half of the view from the bus, and Bhasi took his eyes off as the bus moved on.

Bhasi lived on the outskirts and hence had the luxury of a three-bedroom cottage with a chimney. The house looked like those in the woods, with smoke billowing from the chimney. He stepped off the bus and waved cheerfully before alighting. A ten-minute walk through the side lane, full of rose bushes, led to a small wicket gate. He saw his red-bricked house and smiled to himself. His wife was pregnant for the third time, and they had 2 daughters, Indulekha, aged 3 years, and Chandralekha, aged a year and a half.

Malathi, his wife, was in her late 30s, and hence they were a bit worried about the pregnancy. She, too, was working as an administrator in a grammar school until the last trimester. Malathi's mother is too old to travel to England from India. Bhaskaran is very cheerful, and as self-made as he is, so is Malathi. They managed the first 2 pregnancies by themselves; hence, they were quite confident in their acquired midwifery skills.

Days passed very quickly, and Bhaskaran looked at the markings on the calendar. He noted it was the 10th of July and he needed to make his routine call to his father to find out whether he had received the money without any delay. Anjie would be eagerly waiting too. He suddenly realised, looking at the calendar, that by the time he collected his next pay cheque, Malathy would have delivered their third child.

* * *

Chapter 3

The Cycle Rickshaw Ride by Anjie

10th June 1978, Cochin

There was shrieking chatter and laughter of children, piercing Raghavan's ears. He opened his eyes after a jolt and realised it was the sound of children back from school. He got up from his cot, and before he could stand up, Anjie came running to his room and loudly proclaimed, "Appe, Appe" (grandfather), you won't believe what I did today! Raghavan was not fully awake yet and therefore was in an annoyed mood.

"Po (go), poi chaya kudi."* (Go and drink tea*)

Anjie did not listen to that and was keen on telling the story. Suddenly, her other 3 cousins who are co-passengers in the cycle rickshaw came rushing to his room, giggling aloud. He shouted and said, "Yey po poykke ellaam."* (Hey, go away all*)

Children fear their demure grandfather, as he seldom smiles at them or cajoles them. He will show his concern only when they are sick or go away for holidays to spend their vacations at their respective mothers' villages. Sarojaya and Shyamala (Divakaran's wife) both will be waiting for schools to close to pack their bags. During these holidays, one of the daughters volunteers to take care of Raghavan and Dakshayani.

Anjie could not complete her story as Raghavan did not show any interest. She kept her bags on the teapoy in the verandah and walked towards the kitchen. Sarojaya had placed a porcelain cup of milk and cookies for Anjie, and for her children, 2 steel tumblers of tea on the table.

Anjie always shared her cookies with others as well. She was a blue-eyed, golden-haired Anglo-featured fair girl, but she had wide eyes, the only visible Indian trait on her face.

She wanted to narrate the heroic way she pulled the cycle rickshaw away, without waiting for the rickshaw puller. She searched for her grandma and found her sitting in the backyard making brooms. "Mattamme, ithu kettaaa,"* (*Grandma, you know...)* She told her how the rickshaw puller was talking to another fellow puller, who too was waiting to pick up other students from the school. Both of them were so engrossed in the chat and did not notice the girl pulling the rickshaw away. When the onlookers shouted, only then did he realise that the rickshaw was being pulled away. He had to run behind it for a few yards before he could catch hold of it. The children were all hooraying her cheerfully and hooting at him at the same time. The poor rickshaw puller panicked and was shouting in Malayalam at her, "Missy, missy, please stop, wait, it will topple if you lose balance." He was too worried about the lorries that were plying fast on the road; a bit of carelessness will be a tragedy. Somehow, he stopped it and made her sit along with the other children. Missy Anjie was laughing her heart out, and the children always treated her as their hero. The children now started telling her, "this rickshaw man will complain to our grandfather and we will all get nice whacks." Anjie was not bothered, and she herself triumphantly rushed towards their grandfather to narrate the great rickshaw adventure.

Raghavan will always be waiting for them at the gate without fail, but as he went for his usual nap a bit late, he was not at the gate.

Children heaved a sigh of relief and grinned at the rickshaw puller, then ran inside. The rickshaw puller, in turn, said that tomorrow he would complain to their grandfather and made a U-turn before pulling over to exit the lane.

Dakshayani heard the story and warned Anjie of the dire consequences if grandfather comes to know about this and continued her broom making. Luckily, on that day, Raghavan was waiting for Bhaskaran's call, and Anjie also spoke to her father at length and narrated her rickshaw adventure in English, so that grandfather would not get a clue. Bhaskaran had a hearty laugh and after listening to her patiently, told her not to repeat it again as it might endanger their lives. She promised him that she would not repeat this, upon her daddy.

Anjie was a bubbly little angel as her name denotes, that her adventures are as many and are classic enough to be compared to *The Adventures of Tom Sawyer*. She came back to her grandfather's house and drank the cup of milk that was kept for her, changed into a frilled frock, and waited for the tuition missy. At 5 pm, her home tutor would come and help her finish the homework. She was not interested in studies and half of the time would be looking around. At times at the pigeons or at those nests on the golden shower tree. The weaver bird was happily passing some food to the chicks inside, and Anjie suddenly took her eyes back. The day she was brought to this faraway land by her father, she cried a lot upon seeing the strange faces around; then her younger aunt Rema carried her to show this weaver bird nest. Little Anjie forgot everything and keenly looked at the nest and started smiling. Her father stayed for one month and enrolled her in the convent school before he left for England. Sarojaya was a kind-hearted lady and took care of Anjie as her own child after Rema got married. Eight-year-old Anjie again cried unstoppably when Rema left with her husband and tried to console herself looking towards the weaver bird nest; that time it was vacant too.

After her tuition, grandpa will make the children sit for daily prayers in front of the traditional lamp. It is his habit to light the traditional lamp with wick and oil daily, which will be kept ready before dusk. He promptly makes Saro rub and polish it every Friday. Sarojaya started to make her daughters do such chores. The prayers were taught by grandpa, and he too will sit and chant with the children so that they learn it by heart. The children were very disciplined in behaviour too; they had proper guidance from their grandfather, and he monitored their activities very keenly. She will go to her own room in the next-door terrace house, where her father's brother Divakaran and his wife Shyamala and daughter Sheela too lived. Then she will sleep in that house, in her room, to wake up to the alarm at 6 am. After taking her bed coffee given by Shyama aunty, she will get ready to go to school. Her breakfast will be kept ready in the grandfather's house. She will then keep her school bag on the sofa and rush to have breakfast. Her breakfast was always cereals and milk and cut fruits or sometimes bread toast. She tries one or 2 Indian dishes some days, pecking from her cousin Romila's plate. Anjie too started slowly liking idli and chutney or "puttu"* and kadala* curry (Puttu is basically tubes or rolls of rice flour enveloped with fresh grated coconut that are steamed and eaten along with chic pea curry). Sometimes Sarojaya makes pancake for her, which she learnt from Bhasichettan, just to make Anjie eat something during her early days of arrival. First time Bhasi showed Sarojaya how to beat an egg coarsely along with butter, sugar, all-purpose flour (Maida), baking soda, and milk, and then spread it on the pan. Later, Sarojaya tried it by herself; sometimes it got burnt and at times was not cooked properly. Later, Sarojaya gained expertise to make perfect pancakes. The problem was to make homemade butter; she knew only to make perfect ghee and homemade butter always had moisture in it, which made the pancake soggy. Still, she used to make it mixing ghee, and Anjie relished it that way too. Her father used to bring Danish butter biscuits for her while he visited her from the UK. Once she finished it, Raghavan will get local cookies for her from the English bakery in Jew Street.

Bhaskaran's visits have shrunk to once in 2 years after his second marriage. Anjie was eager to see her younger siblings, so every 6 months her father would send her photographs of his new family, which were a valuable treasure for her. She used to take them to school and show them to her friends with pride. They all used to ask her why she looked quite different from her family, so she eventually stopped showing them. But she wanted an answer, and one day she asked her father the same question. He laughed and showed her in the mirror, "Look at the shape of your eyes; you look like me. In fact, if your hair is black, you would look exactly like Rema, your youngest aunt." So, one day, Anjie decided to try this technique. She thought black ink would be a good way to colour her hair black. She had seen the Chepauk blue ink bottle in her grandfather's almirah, and at times he gave money to the rickshaw wallah to buy a new ink bottle. Anjie decided to try her luck on the way back from school. She told him to stop near the Pen Mart and that she needed to get a black ink bottle for grandpa. The rickshaw puller stopped, and Anjie said she would get it. Anjie borrowed money from him to buy the ink. She also told him she would repay him the next day and kept the bottle in her school bag.

As usual, grandfather was standing at the front gate, and she kept her fingers crossed that the rick uncle would not ask for money from grandpa now. The other children were not aware of her plans, and none said anything. As lady luck smiled at Anjie, the rickshaw puller forgot to ask about the ink bottle. Her grandfather looked at her silent face and asked if she was alright. She answered that she was hungry, which is why she looked tired. Anjie donated her cookies to her cousins so that they would sit there munching on them, allowing her to try her hair colouring. She rushed to her room, closed the doors, took out the ink bottle, but she could not open it without someone's help. So, she took it to Shyamala to have it opened. Shyamala, who was sewing something, said the clothes would get smudged with ink if she opened it, so she advised Anjie to take it as it is to her grandfather. Anjie was disappointed and was thinking about how to open it. She stepped out of the house and saw a passing cyclist. She waved at him, and seeing a doll-like little girl waving at him, the cyclist stopped and, upon her request, opened the ink bottle for her. After her successful mission, she jubilantly went back into her room. She carefully opened the ink bottle and poured it into her left hand, similar to how Aunt Rema used to apply oil to Anjie's golden tresses. Anjie then applied the ink to her head. The ink flowed down her fair cheeks and smudged into her white uniform shirt, making a mess. Anjie was a bit panicked and realised her hair colouring mission had failed. She removed her shirt, wiped her hands and cheeks with it, which spread the ink more over her whole face. She changed into her frock, which also got stained with ink from her head. She sneaked out of her bedroom to go to the bathroom without being noticed by Shyamala, but just then Shyamala looked up from her tailoring machine and saw Anjie smeared in ink. "Deivame ithenthu kolam* Anju" (Oh, what is this *), she called her "Anju". "Sorry, Shyama aunty, I wanted to colour my hair black," and she narrated the incident at school and her father's reply. Shyamala started to laugh aloud uncontrollably; it was such a hilarious sight. Anjie was about to cry, fearing her grandfather's wrath. Shyamala helped her wash her hair, and the uniform shirt was soaked in water with washing soda. However, Anjie's face had to be scrubbed many times as the ink was not entirely gone. One side of her face looked like a ripe tomato, and Shyamala couldn't control her laughter again. Then, grandfather came looking for her as the tuition teacher was waiting. Seeing Anjie's face, he was shocked, and Shyamala explained the whole episode. Grandfather was so angry and said, "Oh oronnu oppikkum arampurappu*" (This naughty girl creates one thing or another*). He didn't say anything further as the tuition teacher was waiting at their house. Anjie took it as a chance and rushed to get away from her grandfather. Shyamala narrated the story to Bhasi and Divakaran during dinner time, and all had a hearty laugh. Bhasi was supposed to travel to Goa with his friends and was getting ready; he would be flying to London from Goa via Mumbai. His younger brother, Krishnan, who was a sailor, would also meet him in Mumbai. Krishnan, along with his wife Premila and 2 children, was staying in Malad, in the apartment earlier leased out by Bhaskaran when both brothers were bachelors in the early 60s. Bhaskaran was a typist in a shipping company (logistics), and Krishnan, who was just 18, was brought to Bombay by Bhaskaran and enrolled in a shipping institute for a certificate course to become a sailor. Bhaskaran later managed to go to England after marrying Margaret, a widow with one son who was the private secretary of the then Managing Director of the shipping firm where they were employed. The kind-hearted

British-origin Managing Director sponsored Bhaskaran so that he could accompany his wife to England.

Anjie was again asked to smear some oil on her face before sleeping, so the next day she could again scrub her face thoroughly to remove the ink. Bhasi left for the airport before daybreak, and while planting a kiss on his sleeping daughter's forehead before leaving, his lips murmured, "My poor child," and tears rolled down his cheek.

Anjie got up to get ready for school, but her face was smudged with ink traces. Shyamala told her to stay back for a day and informed the rickshaw puller that she would not be coming. "Missy Kku sughamille?" (Is Missy unwell?) the rickshaw puller asked. She briefly narrated the previous evening's events. Banu Lal, the rickshaw puller, explained to Shyamala how she bought the ink and he paid for it. Shyamala asked him to get the money from Raghavan, and he replied that he would collect it in the evening.

Shyamala came back after seeing off Sheela and told Anjie about it. Anjie was now sure that grandfather would punish her for this. In the evening, Anjie had no other way but to face him as the home tutor would come to teach her. She had made Shyama aunty bring her lunch pack to her room from grandfather's house so that she could avoid facing him. Shyamala too obliged as she too did not want the little one to get thrashed.

But in the evening, grandfather was waiting for her to come and sit for tuition. He took a cane from his almirah and gave 2 thrashes on Anjie's calf. She stooped down and looked down, her eyes fixed on the ground, without raising her neck to look at him.

Grandfather said this whack is for doing things on her own, for cheating the rickshaw puller by telling lies. Tears rolled down her cheeks, and even Tuition Missy felt bad; her cousins sat with a saddened face and none looked up.

But melancholy was not to stay in Anjie's mind at all. She will again find some way to keep herself entertained and wanted her cousins to continue the hero worship. This time it was the next-door neighbour's chance, who had to go hungry due to Anjie's shenanigans. There was another house between Anjie's father's and grandfather's houses. This house was literally built utilising all available space, and due to this, the kitchen window was an open-type hollow round gap on the boundary wall, towards the roadside. It was kept to let out the smoke from the kitchen stove. In those days, the mud stove in which firewood was burnt was used for cooking. Anjie used to watch keenly the smoke whirls coming through the circular gap. One day she saw a kitten jumping out through that gap and meowing at her. From the next day onwards, Anjie carried a cookie in her hand and started feeding it while going to her room after her supper. The kitten too started waiting for her, sitting in the hollow space licking its paws. The kitten would eat the cookie and then rub against Anjie's feet with gratitude and meow. One evening, Anjie did not find the kitten in its usual place. She mockingly meowed too, yet the kitten didn't appear. Anjie thought it would be inside sleeping, so without knowing the time, she took some sand from the road and threw it through the gap into the house. Yet the kitten didn't turn up. Unaware of what she had done, Anjie sadly went to her room. The consequence of her sand-throwing act was another whack for her with Grandfather's cane. Sarojaya, who usually supports

Anjie, this time said she deserves it as the next-door neighbour couldn't eat supper as the rice was full of sand. Apparently, the sand thrown by Anjie landed in the rice which was boiling in the stove.

Anjie explained it was not intentional and it was only to beckon the kitten outside. The neighbour, Lalitha Bhai, had just taken the kitten and placed her under a woven basket so that her fish curry would be safe from it. The handful of sand thrown was seen all around the mud stove, and they could sense what would have happened. They promptly complained to Raghavan, and he was boiling with anger at Anjie. Anjie stopped giving a cookie to the kitten and started throwing stones at it if she sees it on the road. The kitten has now become a cat but still it runs away as soon as Anjie was in sight.

The rains are too dirty in Fort Kochi as the uncovered drains just overflow, and it is so filthy to even walk on the road. Those were the times when scavenging people were called to remove the blockages, and to make things worse, they scoop out the entire filth from the drain but keep it on the sides of the roads. The mosquitoes swarm everywhere and spread Elephantiasis all over. Anjie's grandmother, Dakshayani, too was infected by this disease; she had 2 oversized legs, too heavy for the lady to walk freely. She too once heard her father referring to Divakaran that Malathi is scared to visit Cochin due to all these.

* * *

Chapter 4

The Matrimonial Advertisement

England, 1973

Bhaskaran was living in a one-room apartment near the County court after he divorced Margaret. He started living alone immediately after returning from India, leaving his daughter there. Despite his solitude, the apartment was very cosy for him and was kept neat and clean always. Bhaskaran was as disciplined as his father and had a similar way of doing things. The apartment had a modest decor with wooden flooring and a proper heating system. It had a centralised heating system, the greatest invention of those times that replaced the coal-fed chimneys. He was told by the realtor that the heating system used here was by steel and aluminium radiators. He was surprised to see the huge Radiator room in the basement where things were meticulously operated, a moment he was proud enough to be a consumer of a gadget, an output of modern invention. Bhaskaran was a fairly good cook as he used to cook Indian dishes all the while since he left his hometown at the age of 19, and he continued cooking in his first marriage too.

After his divorce, Bhaskaran was too bored with life. Moreover, as he was only 40 years old, he started thinking of a second marriage. He saw a matrimonial advertisement in an

Indian paper which arrived every week from India by post. The alliance read, "Seeking alliance for a 32-year-old postgraduate, convent-educated woman. NRIs are preferred. Caste and marriage status no bar." This was a good match for Bhasi, so he immediately wrote back giving all his details. He even provided his younger brother Divakaran's telephone number in Cochin. They had a pricey telephone connection in their home so that Bhasi could make trunk calls from England to talk to Anjie. This was a rare thing in those days, and in Cochin, only a few businessmen had their own telephones. The black telephone was kept on a cradle, was a rotary type, and the dial had numbers 0 to 9 on it. One had to put an index finger into the dial and complete the full circle to make a call. To complete calls, one needed to dial all the numbers by inserting fingers into the dial where each corresponding number was placed, following the same pattern as above. It might take a few failed attempts to get connected. Many times, it would end up with wrong numbers, which would also be metered.

Apart from sending money to his father, he used to send some money bi-monthly to his brother too, to maintain the joint property and the telephone. His brother had already returned from Bhutan and was doing a small business selling antiques in Jew Street area. The telephone was sporadically used to make outgoing calls as it was quite expensive in those days. The three-digit number 301 was very easy to remember as well. In order to book a trunk call, Bhasi had his own connection in the small apartment in England too. He was a hardworking person and had clean habits, except for the occasional social drinking. The white wine, manufactured in 1900 in Denmark as the trade dress on the bottle claims, was gifted by his colleagues for his 40th birthday. It was displayed on a pretty horse cart model wine holder made of leather. It was the only showpiece in his apartment. He was told that the wine must be kept in a bottle slanted at a 45-degree angle always to keep the natural ageing process going on. Hence, he paid a good price for the wine holder to preserve this pricey gift.

Thus, the alliance took off and he travelled to Bangalore where he got his marriage registered. He was constantly in touch with Malathi over letters and through a couple of phone calls before they decided that both were compatible. As soon as Malathi secured a job, they both moved into a more spacious apartment in the same building with one more bedroom; both girls were born in that apartment. They planned to buy a house in the suburbs and saw advertisements of realtors dealing with it. It took a year of house hunting before they could find this red-bricked cottage. The realtor mentioned it was earlier owned by "Shakunthala Devi", the living computer. Bhaskaran did not probe further into it as he thought it was not necessary and it might be a sales pitch by the realtor to increase the saleability of the cottage, as the prospective buyers are Indians.

Both of them took out a joint mortgage and bought it in joint names too. All was not as smooth as it seemed; petty egos clashed almost daily between them. They still decided to try for one more child, expecting a boy this time. Malathi never bothered to talk to little Anjie nor enquired about her husband about her, for Anjie was not part of her family. This was understood in her deeds, and Bhasi too accepted it that way so as not to break the peace.

* * *

Chapter 5

Anjie's "The Thing"

1983, December, Cochin

Anjie started a membership at Eloor lending library when she was 13. Her three friends were her classmates at Holy Angels. They too enrolled in the library just because Anjie wanted them to. One is Kalindi Solanki, called Kallu, the daughter of a Gujarati merchant who was running a textile shop in Ernakulam town and had a few other businesses. The second one is Ruth Thomas, the daughter of Dr Thomas and Dr Cecilia, who run their own medical clinic in Thoppumpadi. The third one is Mahalaxmi Bhat, the daughter of High Court lawyers Narayana Bhat and Arundhati Bhat.

There was a Jewish girl named Martha, who was a bit shy type and her father was the Rabbi of the Jewish synagogue, her mother a homemaker. Martha was but just a namesake friend for them. As she was very conservative, she never joined for sleepovers, yet they included her in the gang. Her father had applied to go to Israel like all other Jews who had done 'Aliyah' (immigration) to the newly formed Israel. The Jews all over the world had started opting for immigration since it was formed in 1948. So, at any time she would move away from them. For the Jewish festival Hanukkah, her mother invites all her friends home on the evening of the 8th day of celebrations. It usually falls during the last week of November or the first week of December. It differs each year as the Jewish calendar and Gregorian calendar do not always corroborate.

She will light up the nine-branched menorah with 8 candles every day and add the ninth candle on the last day of celebrations. They display it on the windowsill so all the passersby can see it. The main dish she cooked was potato wedges. After the 'Sabbath' is over, she will serve them dinner and ensure all are dropped back home in their ambassador car. The car started with a roaring sound and emitted a burning petrol smell that pierced one's nostrils. Anjie loved the smell though.

All 5 of them were partners in crime and thick friends. They all wore miniskirts and high-fashion frocks, their hair cropped in the latest style, which proclaimed their rich upbringing. Every weekend, Anjie would come for a sleepover at one of their houses accompanied by the other 2, depending on whose house they were spending the weekend at. All their families were always welcoming too. Every weekend, all 4 ensured that they stayed together. Cecilia, despite her busy schedule, would ensure that on the weekend visits of Anjie, Kallu, and Maha, she herself cooked special beef fry or cutlets for Anjie. Maha and Kallu were vegetarians. Anjelina enjoyed this special attention she was getting from Ceci aunty.

At times, Dr Ceci had to rush to the clinic if any ladies were in labour and would return late and tired. Anjie and the others would be dropped back home on Saturday evenings, and Anjie would wait for a month again to reach Aunt Ceci's home, the home she loved most. The huge bungalow, known as "Kappal Veedu", in the neighbourhood stood on Appakkaran Street.

This was built by Varkey Moplah, the father of Dr Thomas who was a spices merchant in those days. The grandfather's life-size portrait was hung on the wall of the drawing room with a certain air of commanding poise in his eyes too.

The house was built in European architecture. The large portico is suspended at the height of approximately 5, six-foot people on top of each of the 4 cylindrical pillars. These pillars had an entwined Bougainville creeper which was full of paper-like dark pink and white flowers. There is a balcony overlooking the car porch downstairs, and children will come rushing to the parapet of the upper-level balcony. If they are playing on the wooden horses kept there, they can hear the sound of car engines coming inside the gate. All of them will then rush down the stairs to greet Dr Ceci as she will have some goodies from the French bakery or English bakery for the children. Dr Ceci always wears cotton sarees when going to the clinic, and she was never seen wearing a wristwatch. Later, when Anjie inquired about this, she explained that her kind of work, helping women deliver babies, cannot accommodate a watch or bangles as it consumes time to remove them and wear gloves in case of an emergency. Anjie nodded, even though she could not fully understand it. Anjie always keenly watches Cecilia talking to Ruth and her brothers, Paul and Philip. She used to feel a kind of heaviness somewhere in her chest, unable to precisely describe the emotion. The siblings and Ruth fight a lot for chocolates and cartoon video cassettes. When Anjie visits their house, they allow her to play Michael George Wham and Michael Jackson's video songs. At Anjie's request, her father Bhaskaran bought a video cassette player as a gift for her 13th birthday. Now that she was growing up and starting to show signs of puberty on her body, Shyamala stopped her from going for sleepovers. Anjie could not understand why it should be restrictive to sleep at a friend's house just because one has turned 13. Little did Anjie know what it is to be a girl who turns out to be fully grown. She could hear Shyamala talking to Ceci aunty over the phone, mentioning that "the thing" would start for Anjie at any time, which is the reason for not sending her to sleepovers.

Anjie could not hear what Ceci's aunt's reply was, but she could guess that she too quickly agreed to the point. One day, the much-awaited "the thing" happened to Anjie as expected by her aunts.

Rema had come for a visit to stay with Anjie for a day and take her to Chittoor for the Christmas holidays, where her husband was posted. All set and both packed Anjie's Mills and Boon collections too. Rema was saying it would indeed be heavy to carry so many books. Anjie convinced her, saying she would be bored otherwise, as there is no other pastime in Chittoor. Sarojaya and her children had already packed their bags and left for her mother's house a bit far away from Kochi. Anjie used to accompany her at times or go with Shyamala and Sheela to Shyama aunt's mother's house. If she stayed back without going anywhere, Ceci aunty used to pick her up on Xmas Eve to celebrate Christmas, and it was fun too. The freshly baked cake, homemade grape wine, turkey roast, cutlets, and many other items would be on the dining table. Anjie used to love the laced table cover specially taken out for Christmas; somewhere she had seen the same table setting, déjà vu.

Xmas was a feeling for Kochi, streets full of youngsters dressed like Santa Claus, going up and down to the houses in the neighbourhood. Children used to rush to the gate to see the "pappanjis" as they were locally called. During New Year's Eve, they do have the Kochi Carnival too, but Anjie's uncles never allowed the children to step out as there were drunken brawls in the street and it was very unsafe for ladies and children to be outside. But during carnival times too, they could see youngsters dressed up as the characters of the Hindu epics Ramayana and Mahabharata plying up on bicycles. Indeed, it was a hearty comic sight to see them smoking cigarettes and beedis, grinning their way to the happening streets of Jew town.

Anjie was sleeping with Rema in her room that night, ready to get up early to catch the super-fast to Palghat. But Anjie suddenly started crying in the midnight, which made the entire house wake up. Rema was panic-struck, Shyamala too got up and came rushing to Anjie's room. Divakaran too came behind her, rubbing his sleepy eyes. Then Anjie told Rema that she had terrible stomach pain. Divakaran stepped out to the streets in his vest and lungi itself, to see if any cycle rickshaw was available. He walked into the dark towards the end of the street.

Then suddenly Shyama spotted a red ink mark on Anjie's frock and quickly understood the reason. She whispered to Rema, and both got the point; Anjie got "the thing." It was 5 am, and they made her understand what it is. Though Anjie could not follow everything, she could guess the situation and related it to the red ink smudge on the back of Grace's pony, while Grace was riding it (Grace is the protagonist of a recent Mills and Boon novel which she read, that had this event described).

Rema said this is now going to be a recurring monthly affair and she needs to be prepared for this. Shyamala went inside and got a few sanitary napkins from her cupboard. She explained how it should be tied as a knot and what the string is meant for. Anjie was quite perplexed, and Rema said she would help. Anjie felt so shy that Rema would now break into her privacy, even though she was her own dearest aunt. Anjie then said she could handle it all by herself and asked them to leave her room. She keenly looked at the illustrations on the cover which read "CAREFREE," a beautiful plastic white cover with a few daisy flowers imprinted on it; it looked nice.

Both Rema and Shyamala sat on the front verandah and waited for Divakaran to return. Soon, Divakaran came back with a rickshaw wallah, and Shyamala told him about the incident. He paid the rickshaw puller some money and sent him off. Divakaran's face looked relieved as he switched on the electric pump, part of his daily morning routine. Since it was already 5 am, he decided not to go back to sleep. The 3 of them sat on the verandah and started discussing random topics about the weather.

Rema decided to stay back with Anjie for a week, as Shyamala wanted to go to her mother's house as planned earlier. Rema later went to the Mattanchery shopping street and bought some sweets and a new frock for Anjie.

Anjelina Bhaskaran wore her new frock and stood in front of the mirror, smiling at her own image. But she wanted to cry because Grace in Mills & Boon story cried too when she got "the thing." She recalled how the white pony, which Grace was riding, had its seat smudged with red when Grace dismounted it. Grace had run to her stepmother and cried in that story. For no reason, Anjie started crying, which again made Rema panic-struck. She cajoled her niece, hugging her, and asked if she was having any stomach cramps. Anjie dramatically nodded her head, laid down in her bed, and slowly slipped into sleep. Her dreams featured a dining table covered with a white laced tablecloth. It had designer chairs made by famous Sheraton, Hepplewhite, and Chippendale, which were described as kept in Lord's dining room in Mills & Boons (which Anjie had marked with red ink in those books).

Rema's husband, Babu, also joined her to stay for a week along with Rema as she was staying back. They had been married for 5 years now, but had no children yet. Both will be going back to Chittoor in another 5 days as soon as Shyamala comes back from Guruvayoor.

Meanwhile, Dakshayani had a fall from the cot, and Rema was luckily sitting on the verandah of her father's house at that time. She came near Dakshayani upon hearing her wails but could not lift the heavy lady alone. Raghavan was too fragile to even offer a hand of support. Anjie heard her aunt's voice on the verandah narrating the incident. Babu was having an afternoon nap, and upon hearing this, he rushed to the other house. The old lady was still lying down, unable to get up. Both, with great difficulty, lifted her from both sides and put her onto the cot. Babu telephoned Divakaran's pp number in the shop next to his and conveyed the message. He also asked them to tell Divakaran to arrange an ambulance to shift her to the hospital. Their elder sister's daughter was working in a laboratory in Thoppumpady. Divakaran asked her to arrange an ambulance immediately, she did so, and incidentally, it was Dr Ceci's clinic's ambulance. The hospital staff too had come to shift her to the hospital. Meanwhile, Thangavel had come back after a two-day stay in Saro's house, leaving her and the children there to spend their Xmas holidays. Raghavan asked him to immediately go and fetch them back, as the old lady is now bedridden and Rema needed help. He did not bother to ask Divakaran to bring back Shyamala as he very well knew that Divakaran will not oblige. Sarojaya was surprised to see Thangavel back late at night to her house. Thangavel explained the situation. Sarojaya told her mother about it, and they started packing stuff to take to Kochi – things like dehusked coconuts, tapioca, cocum, tamarind, turmeric, yam, plantain, ripened bananas, long beans, papayas, bitter gourd, etc. – in a gunny bag.

Sarojaya's mother used to pack all these home-grown items and at times coconut oil, gingelly oil, and home-cooked jackfruit halwas too in summer. Now that she must leave immediately due to this emergency situation, she could pack only a few items than usual. The neighbour had a carrier cycle in which he carries fodder for his cattle and, as per Sarojaya's mother's request, he took the gunny bag on his bicycle to the bus stop, which is a mile away from their house.

Thangavel, along with Sarojaya and their children, reached back to Cochin the next early morning. Rema heaved a sigh of relief as she saw Sarojaya and explicitly told her so. Rema mentioned that their sisters-in-law, Radha and Renuka, were in the hospital assisting their mother-in-law and that they needed to take lunch for them. Sarojaya untied the items she brought from home. They both started cutting a few vegetables and set to work like machines.

It was the start of a Herculean task for Sarojaya for the next 6 months, until the old lady passed away.

The mother-in-law was a real terror for the daughters-in-law, especially for Sarojaya as she was the one who stayed in the joint family. Sarojaya had to look after the bedridden lady as well as the household chores too. She requested her sisters-in-law to take turns to come over and stay with their mother who required constant support. Turning the lady in the bed itself to wipe her heavy body was an exhausting task for the people who attended her. While the old lady was on her own, she used to go to the nearby marshland next to the Matha Church and gather some herbal medicinal plants. She would clean those thoroughly, put them in boiling water, and drink for 2 days. Once it was over, she would venture out again to gather fresh ones. When summer started, she would dry these leaves and store them in her almirah to use for the rainy season. Her belief was that her kidneys would get purified because of this and her urine would be as clear as crystal water. Whether it was for all these natural intakes, she did not have any kind of ailments bothering her except her heavy legs, due to elephantiasis. She also got some candles and would light up those candles on the corner of the street where another bylane intersects. She said the spirit of "pranthan kuriachan"* (Name of a Demigod*) was guarding that wall and one should pay respects every evening as they are the residents of that street. She used to tell all her children that this was a practice in that street since they started living there, so no idea about who had started it and what is the basis for such faith. But all residents of that lane followed the same routine. These candle lights were bliss for those who returned home from work during nighttime. Sarojaya and the other 2 daughters-in-law also prayed to "pranthan kuriachan" for their husbands' jobs and financial problems. Raghavan used to laugh at these ladies praying to that wall, and he was clever enough to know why it started; the hooligans would always relieve themselves onto the walls, and this intersection was an ideal point for this. So, unable to bear with the stench, some wise resident would have started the practice. But he too encouraged people to carry on the practice so that the corner would be neat. One day they even saw some people bringing a bottle of arrack as an offering to the spirit who is supposedly living there. This was not entertained by the neighbour, and he chased them away and asked them to take back their offerings too.

While Dakshayani was suffering to breathe her last breath, Anjie saw her grandfather lighting the candle and praying to the wall with folded hands. The very next day, the lady passed away, and there was a loud cry from the daughters who had gathered around her cot. The death was confirmed by the doctor who came home to certify.

* * *

Chapter 6

Anjie and Cousins

Kochi, 1984 April

Bhaskaran had to go to India to perform the last rites of his mother. He could travel only after 10 days of her death as this summer he had planned to bring Anjie along with him for a couple of months until her school reopened. He had made the arrangements early enough and had informed Malathi about his plans. She too nodded as her children would have company while they both were away for work. The children were excited to see their sister, whom they had met once while visiting Kochi after the birth of their third child, Chithralekha. She is now 3 years old, so all 3 sisters were indeed very happy to hear about it. Bhaskaran set off to Kochi as planned, and incidentally, he could make it for the 16th day rituals of his mother as these dates coincided with his earlier bookings. Anjie started packing her things for her first visit to England since her father had taken her to Kochi.

Bhaskaran's arrival was this time into a gloomy house, where all the siblings had gathered for the 16th-day ceremony. After a couple of hours of tears, hugs, and laments about their mother's painful departure, all of them started their chit-chats as usual, sitting in the Panthal arranged for conducting religious rituals the next day. There was a topic to be settled which the sisters were waiting for Bhaskaran to arrive for. There was a blue addilum pathakkam (necklace) as it is called, which their mother used to wear for the last 50 years. It is quite heavy and looked beautiful. Bhaskaran immediately looked at Raghavan and found his father silent. He got the clue that it was, as you people decide.

Bhaskaran asked the other sisters if they were okay with giving it to Sarojaya, as she was the one who had toiled a lot for their mother. They all unanimously agreed, and Bhaskaran handed it over to Sarojaya.

She just investigated those blue stones and plainly wore them on her plump neck. Her daughters could not control their enthusiasm; they came running near her and took a closer look at the heirloom status-acquired single jewellery piece possessed by the entire family, as if it were the Kohinoor jewel adorning Sarojaya's neck. This time, Krishnan and his wife Premeela had also come from Bombay to attend the functions. They too could not pay their last respects to their mother as they arrived 2 days later after her funeral.

Bombay to Cochin trains were full almost every day, not to mention during summer. They had a terrific journey to reach home by an unreserved compartment. Krishnan and Premi had 2 sons, who are epitomes of childhood naughtiness. Anjie calls them both "Denices the Menace." They all make a gang to cycle around the colony, a few of them hitchhiking on some passerby's cycles as only Anjie had her own Ladybird cycle, which did not have a front bar or a carrier seat behind her Pedaler's seat that is strong enough for another child to pillion ride. They all would beg their grandfather for some money to buy "madammapullu and ice" (dragon beard candy and ice popsicle) from the ice vendor standing on the corner of Jew Street. After haggling with him just to exhibit her talent in front of her cousins, Anjie would always get an additional ice popsicle for the price of 5, thus making it 6.

Anjie had already befriended a Jewish grandmother who lived in the lane next to the synagogue; she was a distant relative of Martha, her friend. Sarah aunty used to sell laced kerchiefs and other embroideries knitted by her and had her studio in her house itself. Apart from kerchiefs, Sara Aunt's studio displayed coasters with crochet work, scarves, kippahs (the traditional cap pinned by Jews on the head), and a few Jewish prayer books in Hebrew. There are always visitors in her house, who are all tourists from Israel and all over the world, who wanted to click pictures with her. Sarah aunt's assistant ensures that all of them remove their chappals before entering her house and need to wash their hands and faces thoroughly with lime grass soap kept near the wash basin fitted for this purpose. Sarah aunt's house was open for all. The visiting hours were strictly from 8 am to 11 am in the mornings and 4 pm to 5.30 pm in the evening.

Once Divakaran had brought Sheela and Anjie to buy some kerchiefs from her. From then onwards, Anjie used to visit her house. The Jewish granny named Sarah Cohen knew her grandfather from young days too.

Sarah's aunt's house was a place where Anjie was allowed to go alone. At times, she misused this permission to meet her Anglo-Indian boyfriend, who owned an antique shop. They would meet in the corner bakery, but Anjie could not enjoy the rendezvous as she knew Divakaran might spot her with this boy if she continued doing it. This friendship did not last too long due to this.

Sarah Cohen, the Jewish lady in town, did not want to leave Cochin when almost all her contemporaries had already gone back to Israel. Some died in Cochin itself, a few died after reaching Israel or while living there, where all of them went back searching for their roots. Israel had acquired a new identity by now, and the administration was welcoming all the Jews spread around the world with a lot of offerings and pensions.

Sarah aunty was brought to Cochin by her parents when she was a 3-month-old baby and has lived in Kochi since then. She says she is 64 years of age and studied in the same school where Anjie is studying. Sarah's husband was a rich tax lawyer who passed away a few years ago, and they did not have children from their marriage. Kochi has always been a place where multicultural people are welcomed and have lived. The synagogue known as Paradesi Synagogue is 500 years old and is a very prominent synagogue in India. It is relatively new compared to other synagogues in India, the oldest being built in Kodungalloor, Kerala. The Jews arrived as early as 67 BC along with King Solomon's traders and traded peacefully along the coasts of India. They were so wealthy that they were given princely status by the Raja of Kochi.

The day came when Anjie and Bhaskaran took the flight to Bombay, where they would wait for 2 hours before taking their international flight to London. All family members came to see off Anjie, and all her cousins and aunts had tears in their eyes. Anjie hugged Raghavan and touched his feet for blessings; the old man too could not hold back tears from his welling eyes. Anjie and her father reached Bombay and got onto their British Airways flight to London.

*   *   *

The Attic Adventures

April 1984, England

Anjie slept for at least 5 to 6 hours and the rest of the time read her Mills & Boon novels, before dozing off again. It took 9 hours to reach London, and it was past 5 in the evening when the flight landed at Heathrow Aerodrome. Anjie was excited to follow her father to the taxi stand, where Bhaskaran had already arranged for one of his acquaintances to pick them up. Bhaskaran's Punjabi friend was running a private taxi service that needed to be booked in advance; it would take 3 hours to reach their home in the suburbs. Bhaskaran was talking to the Sardarji in Hindi, and Anjie dozed off once more. They arrived home around 8 pm, and all 3 of her sisters came running to hug her, even the youngest one, albeit a bit hesitantly. Anjie lifted Chithralekha and gave her a kiss on her rosy cheeks. Malathi also greeted her with a warm hug. Anjie looked at her and asked, "How are you, mummy?" Malathi just gave her a peck on the cheek and instructed the sisters to show Anjie her room. Upstairs, Anjie noticed a new cot had been added to the room shared by Indulekha and Chandralekha. They had pinned all 3 of their names on the door and had included her name as Anjulekha (Anjelina). Anjie was surprised to see that and asked why it was written so. Indu smiled and explained that she wanted a similarity in all their names, hence she had written it that way.

After a quick shower, Anjie came down and Malathi had made Chappathi and Indian curry ready. Anjie was surprised to see the hot dish and asked whether Malathi cooked these; in turn, Malathi replied that a north Indian cook would come every Sunday to make dishes required for another 6 suppers. In the mornings, they have cereals and fruits. In the afternoon, the girls eat at school, and the younger one in the creche. Anjie thought about what she should do for her lunch. As if Malathi read her mind, she showed her some cookbooks and the kitchen items kept in the rack, and told Anjie that now that the schools are closed, she and her sisters need to manage lunch by cooking some simple meals like pasta, etc.

As Anjie was only 15, Malathi said she would boil the pasta in one go and stock it in the refrigerator so that the girls could just mix it with the bacon or boiled potatoes accordingly, adding a bit of seasoning like rosemary, oregano, or garlic. Anjie was entering the world of cooking, which she had never tried back in Kochi. She wished she could bring Aunt Saro to her English kitchen and missed her for the first time.

Anjie was so tired that she could only remember getting herself tucked inside the warm quilt. The next day, in the morning, she woke up to a giggle and found the smallest of the lot near her bed. Chithralekha, with the pet name Chithu, was trying to climb onto her cot and struggled with her little palms to clutch onto the mattress. Anjie helped her up and placed her on the cot. The little one gave an accented thank you, which made Anjie thoughtful about her own second year of birth; she too would have spoken with the same Brit accent for sure. While Chithu started mumbling her own stuff, Malathi, dressed up for the office, came to Anjie's room and handed over a slip, a ready reckoner for her use of things at home.

She just picked Chithu and said she had to rush after dropping the little one at her day care.

Anjie wondered where the other 2 had gone, as they were not seen in their beds. She got up and opened the window, looking towards the front yard, and saw Malathi's car going out of the gate, turning left, with the rose bushes further blocking her view. The rose bushes were full of blooms, pink-coloured blooms that were a visual treat and reminded her of Saro auntie's mother's place. There was a huge rose bush full of blooms next to the well in her home in the village.

She quickly went to the washroom and got into one of her frocks from her luggage and rushed down. She did not see her father anywhere, but her sisters were in the kitchen trying to arrange the breakfast table. Anjie was curious at first to watch them, but suddenly remembered she was not a guest here and needed to help them out.

"Hey ladies, how can I help you?" Anjie hugged Chandra, while patting Indu on her shoulders.

"Anjie, today we shall make breakfast for you, and tomorrow you should make for us, okay?" Anjie nodded in approval and reclined on a sofa next to the dining table. "By the way, where is daddy?" she asked.

They replied that daddy leaves for work promptly at 8 am and mamma leaves at 8.20 am. If they had school, they too leave by 8 am, as their school bus comes promptly by that time. All of them will be back only by 6 pm as the girls will stay back in school until that time for after-school activities. Indu plays badminton and table tennis. Chandra is into horse riding and swimming.

Anjie suddenly remembered that in her school no such activities were there, named as after-school activities except for the regular sports curriculum. She wished she could do all these and was thinking about the cool girls of her Mills and Boons. For no reason, she felt sad and missed the weaver bird nest. She remembered a story of Jonathan Livingston the seagull, taught in McMillan English text, wherever it goes seeking happiness, he misses every other place which he left. Finally, he comes back to the place where he belongs to, "The earth." Anjie suddenly turned philosophical and interrogated her mind with the same unanswered question, where do I really belong to?

Girls quite liked the company of their half-sister, despite no common resemblance, though they tried hard to find one. Indu and Chandru, as they were called at home, always looked at Anjie's blue eyes and wondered how their sister from India got these beautiful eyes resembling a gemstone, while they, who lived in England, had dark black eyes. At least brown would have been more acceptable, they once discussed with Anjie. She too did not have a proper answer to their query. One day, while doing a bit of gardening, Anjie saw a small window near the chimneys of the cottage. Contemplating a bit, Chandru said, "Anjie, shall we climb up to the attic?"

Anjie was curious too, but she did not know that it was a formidable place for children, and that was the unwritten rule by Malathi. Chandralekha and Indulekha giggled, winking at each other. The 3 of them, led by Chandru, found their way up to the attic in no time. In their hurry, they left the garden tools on the lawn itself in a scurry to explore the attic.

The attic was a little bit dark and just had the height of a man of 6 ft to stand alertly, not to hit his head on the ceiling. Anjie tried to open the window, and it just opened with a cracking noise, hanging on the single hinge. "Oh no!" exclaimed Chandru, "they will now find out we have come up."

Anjie turned around and asked, "Who will find out?"

Chandru and Indhu said their parents never allowed them up and have told them not to venture into the attic when they were alone.

Anjie was a bit surprised by the rule and wondered why the girls had hidden it from her before climbing up. Anyway, she decided to continue exploring the place and started curiously looking at the dark corner where things were dumped. Her eyes became accustomed to the dim light coming through the single window that she had seen from the garden. The things included some old leather jackets wrapped in newspaper, kettles, a broken chair, some faded crockery, and a few files full of old papers. Anjie saw one doll that was almost worn-out and picked it up. She wondered if it was hers and tried to recollect a memory from it in vain. Suddenly, she found a set of old laced curtains, the same lace that used to catch her eye wherever she saw it, and in her reveries and dreams.

Her curiosity had no bounds, and she tried to pull out the bunch, but it was tied tightly with a thread that her little fingers could not untie. So she left it halfway and started ransacking other stuff. From the pile of a few broken frames without any photos, she found one with a photo of a family. She immediately recognised the young man in the picture as her daddy. Along with him in the picture was an English lady and a little girl, perhaps 3 to 6 months old in her lap, and a boy aged maybe 10 years. She stared at the picture and decided to take it down. Meanwhile, her sisters had left her in the attic and fled. She carefully found her way down. She came to her cot and got the photo removed from the frame without tearing it. She wanted to show this to her father immediately but felt it would be inappropriate at this time, especially when he is with his new family. Anjie started examining the picture carefully and was trying to figure out if the cute baby with cat eyes is herself. How much she wished she knew the people in the picture. Anjie kept the photograph in the side pouch of her luggage bag and started looking at it whenever she was left alone. During the daytime, it was quite difficult for her to sneak out from her sisters as one of them would come in search of her always. One Sunday, Daddy announced that they would be visiting Buckingham Palace that day, and Anjie needed to be shown around London city too.

All of them set out in 2 cars with Daddy and Mummy driving separate cars. The rule is such that the baby must be tucked in a baby seat in the back seat and only one person can sit next to it, so all her sisters were in Mummy's car and she got a chance to be with Daddy alone in his car. Anjie had taken the photo with her and thought even if it is going to make her Daddy angry at her, she has every right to know about the people with him in the photograph. They started the drive, and Daddy started playing Hindi songs in his car and started singing along with Mohammed Rafi. Anjie knows all the legendary Hindi singers through Divakaran and his friends, who visit their house on the weekend for singing and a bit of social drinking too.

When Anjie was declared a big girl after she got her "THE THING," Aunt Shyamala discouraged this meeting and they all started gathering in the shop of Divakaran in Jew Street. She had heard many times Divakaran's story about how he had gone to meet the Legendary Mohamed Rafi and had waited 3 days outside his bungalow in Bombay. Rafi sab used to go out for recording at sharp 8 am and would be back at 9 pm or maybe even later. So, Divakaran would be standing next to the watchman when he opened the gate and salute. With 3 days' acquaintance with the watchman, he came to know that Rafi Saab would notice him if he stood there for at least a week; sometimes he might even stop and talk to him too. Interestingly, according to Divakaran, he used to entertain these watchmen by singing Rafi Saab's songs like "Soja Raja kumari, soja…". Suddenly her thoughts got interfered by her daddy's voice, "Do you like these songs, dear?" Anjie just nodded and went back to Divakaran's narrative running in her mind. At last, on the 7th day, Rafi Saab waved at him and called him inside. He invited him to the drawing room and in Divakaran's words, "njan virakkenerunnu, enthu parayanamennarinjooda*" (I was thinking what to talk*?) and all his friends eagerly waiting to hear what Rafi sab asked him. He asked him where he was from and when Divakaran replied that he was from Fort Kochi, Rafi sab asked whether he knew Babu Raj, the legendary gazal singer. Divakaran showed the photo in his wallet with Babukka as everyone called him, so Rafi sab patted on his shoulders and told him to return to Cochin and not to waste time loitering in Bombay.

This made Divakaran return to Cochin, and later he found a teaching job in Bhutan and left for Bhutan.

Bhasi's humming sound woke her up from reverie, and then Anjie slowly pulled out the photograph from her skirt pocket and kept it on her lap, which suddenly caught Daddy's attention. He didn't immediately react, though his face turned pale. He patiently said, without any question from her, "It is your mother, Margaret, and your brother, John, but now Daddy doesn't know where they are. Please put it inside your pocket itself and don't show your sisters now; they are not old enough to know these stories." Anjie did not hear anything further that Daddy was saying. Tears were rolling from her eyes without her even knowing. Bhaskaran could not do anything, but he too was weeping; both got immersed in their own world. She just wanted to complete the picnic somehow, reach back to her cot, and see her mother's face. She was happy indeed that she could at least have a face to think of when everyone talks about their mothers. She wanted to return to Cochin and show all her friends her mother's photo.

They all came back home and the only thing that remained in Anjie's mind from the picnic was Charles Dickens' grave inside Westminster Abbey.

Holidays just passed quickly, and she ventured to the attic a few more times when her sisters had their ballet classes. But she could not find anything that might help her further probe the whereabouts of her lost family.

A week before she was leaving for India, Bhasi asked her to accompany him to the Court as her sisters had started school by that time and she would be left alone at home. He could also introduce his first daughter to his colleagues.

Anjie was excited too, as she thought she could get some clues from his colleagues about her mother, Bhasi's estranged wife. She had a bit of a boring day while the court was functioning, and then in the afternoon, she was treated to doughnuts and pastries by the Court stenographer, Maggie. The surprise for Anjie was when her Daddy plainly introduced her as "this is Margarette." Anjie had her jaws open with awe, but Bhasi realised her dilemma and continued, "Yes, she shares your mother's name." Maggie was very sweet to her, and Anjie kept staring at her to find out if her father was trying to dupe her again. She was convinced only when Maggie spoke to her about her family. Maggie was a spinster and lived with her mother. She gave Anjie an old photograph of herself, which Anjie wanted; she had seen it while Maggie opened her wallet to pay at the bakery, writing her address behind it, and told her, "Maybe one day when you grow up and return to England for good, you can visit Maggie aunty, if she is still alive then too."

Both hugged each other and Anjie returned home with all the gifts she had received to take to India and started packing her bags. Anjie took out Maggie's photograph, tucked it into her journal, and wrote down her address in it.

Some peace came to her mind, and she was travelling back to Cochin via Mumbai, all alone, where she will meet her uncle and her cousins. She will stay with them for a few days, and Krishnan uncle will again put her on the airplane alone to fly back to Cochin. The day of the return journey arrived, and even Malathi's eyes were moist as she hugged her. Anjie could hear her whisper, "God bless you, dear."

All 4 of them formed a circle and hugged together. Anjie left her father's house with a heavy heart, and Daddy and Anjie did not talk to each other until she was dropped at Heathrow airport. Bhasi did not take off his shades, so that Anjie would not see his welling eyes. The assisted travel was opted for, and Anjie was taken care of by the Airhostess, who made her feel comfortable throughout the journey.

* * *

Chapter 8

Anjie and Her Treasure Hunt

June 1984, Bombay

The flight landed at Santacruz Airport, Bombay. The airhostess accompanied her to the lounge where Krishnan and his family were waiting. Her cousins were excited to host Anjie in their small room, which they had cleaned thoroughly for their hero cousin. Anjie was a bit tired but still described London and the places she visited. The boys eagerly listened to her narration and asked permission from their mother to take her out to their friends who live in the next building in the same compound. Prameela declined and told them not to disturb Anjie. The boys left to play outside with their friends, leaving Anjie alone. She took out the photo and looked for her uncle. He was lying on the couch in the hall. Anjie nudged him and showed the photograph. He looked at it and smiled. She explained how she got it. Uncle Krishnan went into his bedroom and brought a small envelope in which he had preserved a few old photographs of himself. He pulled out one where he was seen along with Margaret and Bhasi. Anjie was overwhelmed to see one more picture of her mother, even though it looked similar to the one she already had. She insisted he talk about her mother and her mannerisms that he had seen. She said her father was tight-lipped about it. Krishnan was confused and thought for a second before he started talking about her. He described how she used to wear miniskirts and how he felt shy seeing her in that attire. He narrated how he used to teach her son to play marbles and how he had gifted him all his marble collections, which he had received from the soda factory of a neighbour in Cochin. Margaret insisted on going to a studio so they could all have a photograph for remembrance. As far as Krishnan knew, she was a sweet lady with sophisticated manners. Anjie, for the first time, felt angry towards her father for not continuing to live with her mother. Krishnan told her he could show her the building where her parents had worked, even though that company is defunct now.

Angelina could not believe her ears. She planted a sweet kiss on his cheek and excitedly went inside the kitchen where Prameela was cooking food for them.

When she heard from Anjie that where they are going, she raised her brows and came to the hall and asked Krishnan if that was necessary. Krishnan replied, "She should know about her roots, Premi. Poor girl, let her at least see the places where her parents initially spent their time together." Premeela nodded in approval and went back to the kitchen.

Anjie and Krishnan set off on his LAMBI scooter, Anjie tightly holding on to her uncle with both her hands. She was too excited to notice the happenings in the street or the busy Bombay life fast forwarding by her side.

Krishnan stopped his scooter in front of a Victorian-type building, which resembled the type she had seen in London. They alighted and started walking inside the building. While climbing the steps, he said it is on the first floor. As she touched the iron rails of the stairs, she suddenly got goosebumps and thought her mother would have touched these rails around 2 decades ago. Anjie tried to hold back her tears and continuously wiped them with her handkerchief. Tears rolled relentlessly down her cheeks, flowing more and more.

Krishnan led her through a small passage and showed a few boards in front of a door; one read WALLACE & CO SHIPPING, Shaw & Wolf Pvt Ltd, and a few more, before Krishnan pointed out the old plaque in marble which read Chettiar & Lloyds company, "EHH!! This is still here," he was so excited to show her the plaque and told her this was the company her parents had worked for together. Maybe the new occupants were unable to remove it as it was engraved onto the marble plaque; if removed, the entrance would be damaged. Anjie's face was now like a ripened tomato after rubbing constantly with her kerchief, so Krishnan could not read out her emotions precisely. He read those again and again, and Anjie noted down the address engraved below it, which was written as HQ Bombay, Branch: 121, Southampton, United Kingdom. She wished she had come here before she left for England.

The huge door was kept open, and behind the reception desk, 2 guys were sitting and sorting out mails. One, as usual, is a South Indian, and Krishnan got to know that he hails from Salem.

Krishnan's wife Premeela is from Salem, and her father is a Keralite who runs a local textile shop there. After the introduction, Muthu Pandian recognised Krishnan's father-in-law and told his family shops at Vijayalakshmi textiles. In a short span, they became familiar with each other and exclaimed, "The world is too small." Meanwhile, Anjie moved a little closer to a notice board that was placed opposite the reception, which had a lot of old notifications pinned to it. One was dated 1972 regarding a company's new address. She could not read it as it was above her eyesight. She called her uncle and pointed it out to him to read it aloud. Her uncle read it and said it was about some other company. The newfound friend, Muthu Pandian, also had his share of information about Anjie and came out from his desk to help them. He said he would open the notice board for them so they could find any required information.

Anjie was so happy about this gesture, and Muthu Pandian brought the keys and opened the glass door of the notice board. Anjie started sneezing as it was full of dust, which had accumulated toward the rim, and it fell first onto her face.

Muthu Pandian said sorry and told that they seldom use this old board to pin the latest information and just pin it all on the open board next to it. Krishnan flipped a few of the notices and found one related to Chettiar & Lloyds. He read it and said, "This is an announcement about the arrival of the new MD in 1964," and he mentioned that her mother was the Secretary of this MD.

She eagerly started copying it in her journal. Muthu Pandian, who was watching her, saw the desperation in her eyes and told her she could keep it with her and no need to return it. There was nothing else in those clips, so they thanked Muthu Pandian and started back. Muthu Pandian called them back and told them he had a few letters in his drawer which had come in the name of Chettiar & Lloyds company as soon as his company, Wallace & Co Shipping, started functioning there in 1975. Anjie's heart started pounding, and her intuition told her that there would be some lead in it. Muthu Pandian opened the last drawer of his table and took out a polyethylene cover from a textile shop which read Mehta Textiles Bandra, and handed over the heavy bunch to Krishnan. He said none from Chettiar company had come there at all after they moved their base back to Karaikudi, Chettinad. There was a dispatch clerk who worked for another 3 months, and he too left the job as he was not getting paid by the defunct company. During that time, he had given the Karaikudi Head office address so that if any registered letters were to be diverted. This girl, who is in search of her own mother, if she can get some clue out of it, there is nothing more than that. He also added that if any leads come to him while he is there, he shall let Krishnan know about it. He had penned down Krishnan's address as well as Raghavan's address in his diary. He also took down the Karaikudi address of Chettiar & Lloyds from his diary's front page and handed it over to Anjie. She took it and placed it carefully in her bag. They once again thanked Muthu Pandian and left the office.

Suddenly, Krishnan said, "I know one more place where your mother and brother used to frequently visit, the famous church in Santacruz in Bombay." Anjie asked if he could take her there too; he said that is where they are going. Anjie again tightly hugged him and silently said, "Thank you."

The Chapel stood with an acquired peace away from the huzzles buzzle of the city, while looking at it Anjie's eyes again got flooded with tears, efflux of thoughts about her mother, a pious English woman who had come to India to work for her living. Krishnan looked at his watch and said it was almost lunchtime, so she could go inside and pray for a while and come back. Both silently walked inside the Parish Hall. Anjie stared at the altar where the sacred cross was kept and thought again about how her mother would have stared at it 15 to 17 years back. She looked at the benches and found the left-hand side was occupied by one lady and assumed that ladies are supposed to sit towards that side, so she sat on one of the benches put on that side and just closed her eyes. Anjie could again feel the warmth of her tears on her cheeks. Krishnan came and touched her shoulders, indicating that it was time to go. Anjie was not brought up as a Catholic, hence she didn't know how to behave inside the church. She just looked at the Altar again and silently followed Krishnan, putting on the footwear which she had kept outside as she used to while accompanying Romila to the temples. The local temple poojaries (priests) were kind enough and they knew her grandfather very well, so no questions were asked about her identity (usually non-Hindus are not allowed inside the temple premises). Anjelina, by her very look, was a foreigner too. Romila used to even offer Pushpanjali in Anjie's name and "Nakshathra". She was told that Rema aunty insisted on finding out Anjie's birth star and took her date of birth to an astrologer downtown. He found it from the old Almanac that February 21st, 1968, was Anizham. The astrologer even said that a lot of hardships are in store for this girl.

Anjie again jotted something in her journal and mounted onto her uncle's scooter, and they both headed back. It was past 3 pm when they reached the flat. Uncle Krishnan was too tired, as was Anjie. Looking at them, Premi gave chilled lime juice which she had kept ready in the refrigerator. Anjie said thank you while gulping it in one single stroke. Premi was eager to know about their trip, but she was a very sensible lady and hence did not ask about it explicitly. Maybe Krishnan uncle will narrate the happenings in the evening or whenever he is at leisure.

*   *   *

Chapter 9

Naval Base Airport

Cochin June 1984

Anji's airplane landed at Cochin Airport, and the air hostess accompanied her to the gate where Divakaran and Shyamala were waiting.

They all reached home, and her grandpa was eagerly waiting for her arrival. He was so happy to see Anjie back, and all her cousins greeted her with loud shrieks. They were all asked to leave her alone and let her rest. Anjie was not feeling an iota of comfort even though she was back in her room. Suddenly, she hated Fort Kochi and the people around her.

She slept until there was a knock on her door. She saw Shyama aunty standing outside and telling her to get ready for school to check her results. The newspaper shows that the tenth results are declared. Anjie was not at all interested in knowing about the results.

Divakaran and Anjie set out for school in an auto-rickshaw. The school was full of parents and students eagerly waiting for the principal to put the results on the notice board. Time was moving at a snail's pace for Anjie and her friends who were all there. Anjie wanted to show them the photograph of her mother which she had with her, but her friends were in an anxious mood to know about their marks. Hence, Anjie thought of telling them the London stories later.

At last, the notice board had the result papers pinned, and girls gathered around it to find their results. A few of them were a bit gloomy, but as the school had already announced a 100 percent pass rate, none was anxious about failing or passing; they were anxious about their marks, which would determine if they could get into a good college for their pre-university course.

Anjie was a good student, and she could secure a first-class in all subjects, i.e. above 60 percent marks. Now that she has got fairly good marks, Divakaran was very happy, and they both started off to break the news to everyone at home.

Meanwhile, all her aunts had gathered in their home to meet Anjie and to hear her London stories, as well as her results.

Anjie wanted to stay back and enjoy with her friends, but Divakaran told her to come back home. Later, she can meet her friends at leisure. She waved goodbye to her friends with a promise to meet at Aunt Ceci's house the coming weekend.

All at home were very happy, and they all bombarded Anjie about her experience in England too.

Anjie got admission to the art subject at a reputed college in Ernakulam, and in no time, she made a bunch of friends in the batch too. Only Kalanidhi joined the Arts group as she was planning to pursue Law after her pre-university.

Martha had already gained admission to Israel, and Ceci aunty made Ruth take a science subject and enrolled her in a college in Bangalore. They all parted ways very soon. Two years of pre-University also passed very quickly.

Shyamala decided to take Anjie to Guruvayoor so that she could visit the temple too. Anjie obliged to make Shyamala aunty happy. They reached Guruvayoor early in the morning, and as they were all entering the temple, a security guard intercepted Anjie and said foreigners were not allowed inside. All of them were shocked, and Divakaran was trying to explain that she is a Hindu. The guards insisted on an Arya Samaj certificate, which none of them understood. Anjie felt a heaviness in her chest again and wanted to cry loudly. She looked into the people's eyes around her, just shut her eyes, and tears rolled down profusely.

Divakaran was shouting at Shyamala and asked her why she had done this to the poor girl. Shyamala too started crying and said she never thought of these things in her wildest imagination.

Few of the devotees who surrounded them saw the scene and started arguing with the security in vain. The security replied that the administrative rule which has been followed for years, even the renowned singer of the Malayalam language, Yesudas, is not allowed to enter the temple, being a non-Hindu. All of them came back to Kochi without entering the temple. The incident was very painful for Anjie, so she booked a trunk call to her father and spoke for one hour, convincing him to get her admission in England. Her father agreed, and they started the process of applying to universities in England.

Anjie got admission to a university in London, and it was time for Anjie to say goodbye to everyone in her college and Fort Kochi too. Anjie's joy knew no bounds.

After she came back from her last vacation 2 years ago, Anjie was totally changed and did not hang around much outside her hostel room. Because of that, she could score high marks, which made her admission process much easier.

The day of her travel arrived, and it was a gloomy day for her grandfather, uncles, and aunts. Her cousins all slept together the previous night, and all of them cried profusely. But somewhere in the back of her mind, she wanted to fly off as fast as she could.

The old man, with his frail hands, hugged Anjie and told her to visit him as soon as her graduation is over. He said, "Letter idanam ketta" (Post Letters). Anjie nodded.

Anjie nodded and literally washed his feet with her tears while she prostrated before him, seeking his blessings. Little did she know she was seeing him in a conscious stage for the last time.

* * *

Chapter 10

Anjie in Her University

September 1987, England

Anjie reached Heathrow and her father was waiting to pick her up. She will be spending a week with them before she starts her college, which is a day's travel from their home. She will be staying in a dorm and will study for the rest of her college degree.

Anjie had a good time with her sisters, and all 3 had grown up quite well and knew that Anjie is their step-sister.

The dorm where she was supposed to share with a British girl had twin beds, a pair of study table and chairs, and 2 wardrobes. The inmate was already there, and as soon as Anjie stepped in, she greeted her. When Anjie started talking to her, the girl suddenly looked a bit uncomfortable and asked her with a frown, "You have an accent? Aren't you a Brit?"

Anjie was shocked, and again, the same heaviness crept into her chest.

She was looking out of the window in search of the weaverbird nest in vain.

Tears came from nowhere, and there was a lump in her throat which choked her words, "Yes."

But you look British," again the girl retorted. Anjie did not know if she was here to narrate her entire life story to a stranger whom she met a few minutes ago to get approval of her British lineage.

Now, again, Jonathan Livingstone the seagull came flying to her mind.

The girl left the room, and after a while, the matron came along with her and explained to Anjie that she would get another roommate soon. The girl packed her things and left Anjie alone in the room. That night was horrible for her; she tucked into the sleep cover to dream about the laced tablecloth and the Xmas menu on the table. Who was that Dr Ceci in a frock? Suddenly, there was a knock on the door, and she woke up to daylight coming in through the windows. There was an orientation class in the hostel before they all set off for the university. Anjie got ready and arrived at the mess on time, as stated in the brochure timing for breakfast.

Two nights, Anjie was all alone in her dorm. On the third day, a girl with golden hair came into her room with a backpack. She felt a warmth at her arrival, and the girl introduced herself as Susanne, her roommate for the next year. Susanne had swapped rooms with the girl who had left Anjie and informed the matron that it was fine to share a room with a person of mixed heritage.

Anjie could sense the lightness in her chest, and both started chatting.

The university was quite interesting, and they made quick friends with their batch mates and had their weekends packed with parties. The mid-semester was over, and Anjie had by that time shared her story with Susanne. Susanne's father was a chemical engineer who was working for some soap company in Central England. Anjie was hoping Susan could invite her to her home during the break. Indeed, Susan could read Anjie's mind, and in no time, both set forth to Susan's house.

Anjie was welcomed by Susan's parents and her granny who had come to visit them from her old age home where she lives. Anjie suddenly thought about her grandfather who still rules the family and lives life king-size in his own way. They all had dinner together and shall celebrate Christmas together before granny goes back to her old age facility.

Anjie wanted to talk to her family in India, and both started walking to the public ISD booth. Anjie spoke to all her cousins, and she was told that nowadays her grandfather keeps himself in his room in the other house. She told them to convey her greetings to him and hung up the phone. Anjie wanted to go to the address written in her journal while in Bombay and was hesitant to open the topic. Moreover, she did not know much about the place either. Looking at Anjie in a contemplative pose, Susan asked her if she was nostalgic. Anjie expressed her wish to go out and find the address. The next day, both went to the post office nearby and enquired about finding out the place. The postwoman who was in charge was out for delivery, and they had to wait for an hour before she returned. The postwoman came back and found the teenagers waiting for her. She tried to read out the address and with a frown said she had no idea about this address, as she had joined this place only a couple of months back. There were chances that the addresses would have changed by now, and maybe old buildings no longer exist there. But she said if they got permission to access the records by paying a small amount, then she could help find the records pertaining to it. The girls were happy to oblige, and they paid the required fee. The postwoman collected the fee receipt, filed it in her records, and went inside the office. After a while, she came out with a hardbound record book and started examining the alphabetical index of the place. She located the address and the new address registered on the page. The girls thanked her and were joyful at their progress. Nancy Drew and her adventures came to their minds, and they giggled all the way back. They narrated the incident to Susan's father, and he said he would accompany them to the address on Saturday, so they did not need to go there themselves. It was already Thursday, and Anjie had to agree, even though the one-day wait was too terrible for her. Friday was a long day for Anjie, and she tossed on her bed before Saturday dawned.

The address that was jotted down from the post office was 20 miles away from Susan's house. The building, comparatively new, did not have any trace of history to it. Though Anjie lost hope upon seeing it, Susan's father entered the lobby, introduced himself to the receptionist, and spoke in a low voice, which Anjie guessed was about her as the receptionist curiously turned towards the girls. Susan's father came towards them and said the owner of this land had entered an outright purchase, and a lawyer's office is involved in the transaction. Susan's father told Anjie that they would just try to get an appointment by gate-crashing the office. The lawyers of the builders were very helpful and tried to locate the owner's address from their files. They spoke to a few others over the phone and mentioned that the owner is no longer alive, and his legal heirs were the ones who had sold it. However, for Anjie's purpose, they doubted if the young generation would be of any help. Instead, they handed over a phone number, which was supposedly of a lawyer whom they had dealt with during the transaction, who aided the employees of the defunct company. This guy had some escrow fund-related queries regarding the labour entitlement of laid-off employees. This was a good clue that their treasure hunt was progressing, and Susan's father was also very delighted. He paid for the time of the law firm and shook hands with the helpful young attorney. They stopped at a telephone booth and called the lawyer, who promptly gave her office address, thinking they were prospective clients for her. They reached a worn-out part of the city with the character of poverty and not as posh as the lawyers whom they met earlier. Anjie was not bothered by the change in the environment as she had a pounding heart that she was trying to calm down.

The building, which was very worn-out, had a few offices with necessities to conduct their businesses. Each table had a telephone with a locked dial pad. The lawyer lady looked very weak and fragile too. She took the details of the employee's name and started searching her record register. She jotted down something from the register, pushed her chair back, and went inside her locker room, probably the one she shared with all the other attorneys who had tables and telephones with locked dials. She took a few minutes and handed over a set of papers to Anjie, wherein the details of her client, Margarette, were shown. The paper was the first page of the affidavit where the address was clearly given, and the bottom of the page had Margarette's signature, which made Anjie's heart jolt a bit. She touched the paper and started crying profusely. Susan also could not control her tears. The old lady attorney too had her eyes welled. It was an emotional scene indeed; they offered a few pounds to the attorney, which she refused to accept. She waved her hands and walked towards her locker again.

Anjie was now almost getting closer to her mother. She saw her mother's signature, which her mother would have personally affixed at the time of filing her claim in court.

* * *

Chapter 11

Anjie's First Job

1989, May

Anjie was attending an interview as a paralegal in an IP LAWYERS' OFFICE in the suburbs of London. Her graduation date was on 22nd July 1989. She could easily complete her face-to-face interview; within half an hour, her final session with HR was completed too. She was happy that she had bagged this job and that it was the next step for her to get into a decent law school without taking aid from her father. Her father was always happy to support her, though at times she felt she should not be a burden to him. Anjie decided to visit her grandfather in Cochin before starting her new job. She booked her tickets with the stipend amount her father had given her to prepare for the graduation ceremony, like buying new clothes and a graduation gift for herself. Anjie was just yearning to see her grandfather as he sounded very frail whenever she called him around every 10 days. He too expressed his wish to see her. Anjie had her graduation ceremony attended by all her sisters, father, and her stepmother. Now that she had time on hand, Anjie thought of her mission to find out her mother. She took out the old worn-out envelopes from her pouch and decided to start with the address written on it. Susanne too offered to join her so that it could be a vacation trip for them together as they are parting ways soon.

Both set off with a backpack towards Southampton. Susanne's mother packed some hot dogs and cheese for the girls, and they decided to head off to the town first. They boarded the train from central London.

*   *   *

The Reunion

Southampton is a port city in the ceremonial county of Hampshire in southern England, which is approximately 110 km away from London.

Upon reaching Southampton, they searched for a decent bed and breakfast place and slept for an hour before they started their quest. The only thing was the age-old address of Chettiar & Lloyds and her mother's Affidavit address. They proceeded to the Head Post Office and enquired about the PO Box number they had with them. The clerk behind the enquiry desk did not raise her head for a long time despite their gentle voices addressing her. Suddenly, Anjie noticed she was engrossed in counting a few pennies in front of her and maybe she did not want to get distracted.

Anjie stood silently watching her complete the counting and then again tried to wish her, "Good evening, ma'am." Now the clerk raised her head and looked at them with raised eyebrows; maybe she did not want to talk at all to preserve her energy for her own children who would be waiting for her back home after a long day of work. Before Anjie could explain, the clerk turned her face away and without uttering a word pointed towards the clock on the wall. The time was half past 5. Anjie got the indication and asked, "Tomorrow at what time, ma'am?" The clerk gestured 8 with her fingers and walked away from her desk. The girls stood there for some more minutes and decided to walk for some time before hitting the bed.

They reached a building with lots of ivy on the wall and suddenly saw the cross on the top of it. They decided to go inside the church. Anjie suddenly thought of the incident at Guruvayoor temple in Kerala; she was hesitant to enter any religious place due to her unknown, rather confused identity. However, she decided to enter this time; at least by her outward appearance, she belonged to this country.

But this is England, no one is bothered about others here, unlike India, especially Kerala, where people are all curious minds or a bit more into the habit of quest, be it positive or negative. It might be a mild version of Voyeurism that was felt everywhere. The habit never dies; the male chauvinism in India is also an aftereffect of being ruled by various rulers and predominantly by rulers with a colonial mentality. The "missies" (as the Brit ladies were addressed by locals in Cochin at that time) from the West were often doing nothing rather than lazing around the houses, ruling and bossing their local house helps, be it male or female. The men who were working as a chauffeur or gardener got used to this bossing around, and they too wanted to emulate their bosses. The way they found to satisfy their alter ego was to be very rude to their wives back at home. The old pattern of households, much before the British era, was such that the wives were the centrepoint of the houses, whereas their husbands were just visitors to their wives' "Tharavadus" (home). Only a few men stayed back at their wives' houses after getting married. The husbands did not have any right over the house or property or children, whereas wives had the upper hand. The first-born daughter of the house became the next heiress of South Indian families; those were the precolonial era, and once the British set foot on Indian soil, they not only showed their wild attitude toward these naïve citizens but also insisted on them following or adapting these methods in their households.

Suddenly, she thought about her own family in Kochi and how patriarchal they are. The aunts who married into the family were often treated like servants, always in the kitchen, cooking and serving the men and children. The men are seen to be much lazier than these hardworking ladies who toil a lot from the moment they wake up in the morning to feed every family member. Back home, Saroja aunty wakes up at 5 am to ensure everyone is served breakfast before the children leave for school. Lunch is neatly packed for all 4 of them and placed on the verandah's teapoy. Sometimes, Anjie forgets to put it in her bag, and her grandfather has to bring it to school during lunchtime. He waits for the lunch bell to enter the school compound and then goes to the school office to call Anjie. When many children developed the habit of forgetting their lunch, the school opened a canteen on the campus, selling mini lunches at a low cost. However, Anjie never had to buy food from the canteen except once or twice when Saroja aunty had to visit her ailing mother. During those times, the household was managed by Shyamala aunty, who would often exclaim, "Oh! Saro onnu pettennu vannal mathi" (*Oh! Let Saro be back soon*).

Anjie, as usual, was traversing on her thoughts when Susanne's voice nudged her back to EAST PARK. Now both decided to walk back to the hotel, which was near a park. Anjie read the name of the park written on the sidewalls: EAST PARK.

While they decided to sit on a bench near the stone-carved sculpture, Susanne exclaimed, "Ohhh! Anjie, look, we are here near the Titanic Engineers' Memorial."

{****The *Titanic* **Engineers' Memorial** is a memorial in East (Andrews) Park, Southampton, United Kingdom, to the engineers who died in the *Titanic* disaster on 15 April 1912. The bronze and granite memorial was originally unveiled by Sir Archibald Denny, president of the Institute of Marine Engineers[1] on 22 April 1914.[2] The event was attended by an estimated 100,000 Southampton residents}

Both eagerly strolled around and read about the short profile of the tragedy of the INS TITANIC that sailed from the port of Southampton in 1912. The wreckage of the ship was found only in 1985, which became a headline worldwide in those days. They headed back to the bed and breakfast dwelling they had checked into.

After a long day, both fell into a deep sleep. Anjie woke up to a knock on the door and rubbed her eyes, still sleepy. The stewardess was standing at the door with breakfast and coffee for 2.

She looked at the wall clock, which was showing 8 am in the morning.

The stewardess was balancing the heavy tray in her hands and impatiently smiling due to the weight of the tray. The stewardess placed the breakfast tray on the side table and heaved a sigh of relief. Anjie too wanted her to leave the room fast so that she could get back to bed. Susanne was still fast asleep; they both got up around 9 am and each took their coffee, which was ice-cold by that time. Anjie looked out of the window; the outside street was now bustling with activity. Men and women in various forms and shapes, dressed up differently but not seemingly fashionable or in costumes in vogue those days in London, were walking busily on the streets. They rushed to and fro like the busy bodies of ants lost in their own world, hurriedly passing each other. They all looked into their wristwatches often to ensure that the time was not moving faster than required by them, as if they could catch hold of it. The daily newspaper was kept along with the tray of breakfast. Anjie took it and glanced through the headlines; there was nothing important except Prime Minister Margaret Thatcher announcing some new policies for the citizens. Both set forth to the post office and found the timid lady behind the counter, this time looking fresh and smiling. She listened to them patiently and asked them to wait; she had gone inside for a while, and Anjie could not hold her breath for too long, her heart started pounding, making her face even paler. Susanne held her hands and rubbed them gently to pacify her.

The clerk came back with the postman of the area. He said he could mark the address on the town map that they were carrying. He marked both the addresses they wanted and also advised them to take the local bus, then start walking after getting off at the spot. Susanne took Anjie's hand and guided her; Anjie followed her as if she were in a trance. Like the children followed the pied piper of Hamelin, she followed Susanne. Susanne took the lead, and they finally stood in front of the address stated in Anjie's mother's affidavit. It was a green-painted British cottage and had a very humble look. The doorbell rang as Susanne pressed the switch outside. Anjie was still in a trance and could hear the doors opening. Suddenly, she shut her eyes and plugged both her ears with her index fingers.

She could hear the footsteps near her and Susanne's voice, "Anjie," she opened her eyes and could hear her saying, "Come, Anjie, she is inside. It was your brother who opened the doors. I have not revealed about you yet." They both walked inside the cottage and sat on the three-seater sofa. Anjie was looking only at the carpet and did not raise her head to look around at all. The wait was over; they heard a lady's feeble voice, and Anjie looked up. Immediately, she saw her mother, a full white-haired, blue-eyed mother of hers standing in front of her. She hugged her tightly and started crying. "Mamma, mama." Susan was prepared with the photographs and she had spotted one of the same photos framed and kept on the walls too. Susanne showed the lady the photographs while Anjie was crying aloud. Suddenly taken aback though, her mother recognised the photos and reached out to crying Anjie. She hugged her daughter tightly and started crying aloud. Hearing the cries, the man, Anjie's half-brother who had gone inside, came rushing out and could not immediately gather what was happening there.

Susan also, with broken words, explained and handed over the photographs and told him, pointing to Anjie, that she is your sister. The man, who looked aged in his thirties, also started crying and joined the hug group. There was a sudden shift of happiness, and after a few seconds, all 3 of them regained their composure. Susan was overwhelmed with happiness. Anjie was surprised to see the laced curtains on the cottage windows and the laced tablecloth like the one she used to see at Aunt Ceci's house. This time she felt happy to see it; the lump that used to creep into her chest was not there. Susan started back home the next day, wishing to see them all soon.

Anjie's brother was a Sailor too and had to start his voyage the next day. He requested a week's extension, and everyone in his office was delighted at the reunion with his estranged half-sister. His name was James Albert, and everyone called him "JO". Mother and daughter were arm in arm, not staying away from each other even for a few minutes, except for their individual bathroom chores. Anjie made multiple phone calls to her cousins but instructed them not to reveal it to anyone, especially to her father. She was filled with hatred towards her father but found solace by reminding herself that she had her loving family in Cochin because of his actions. During the conversation, her cousin Romila mentioned that their grandfather had been very sick and bedridden for the past few days. Anjie stayed with her mother and brother, and they travelled to London to see her off to India to visit her ailing grandfather. Anjie had lots of photographs in her hands to show everyone back in Cochin.

Anjie's mother had small gifts packed for all the aunts and a special gift for aunts Sarojaya and Rema too for bringing up Anjie as their own. The sweater, which was hand-knitted by her mother, was the one she was carrying for her Appa, the beloved grandfather of hers.

Anjie was received by all of them as usual, and she was jumping on the shoulders of Krishnan uncle, though Krishnan could not guess the exact reason for her unbound happiness, especially when her beloved grandpa was on his deathbed.

Anjie rushed towards Grandpa's cot where he was in a semi-coma stage and was only on liquid food. Anjie started weeping profusely, and her tears wetted the old man's face, with some voice coming out of his mouth. Anjie took out the photographs and uttered in a shivering voice, "APPE APPE, kannu thurannu nokkappae*" (please open your eyes and look, Grandpa), "I found my mummy, look, look." Those who were in and around the house rushed to the room. All her aunts, uncles, and cousins gathered in the small room where the old man was gasping. Now her cousins started telling everyone the summary of Anjie's adventure that she had shared with all of them. Anjie's father had also arrived a week back, as the old man was in a critical condition. Anjie opened her bag and took out the hand-knitted sweater and woollen shawl for her grandfather's feet. She could see tears flowing from the sides of his eyes. Anjie then started distributing gifts to all her aunts. Sarojaya and Rema each received one sovereign gold coin, which they could wear as a pendant on their chains, and both were overwhelmed with joy. Anjie did not bother to speak to her father at all, and they both avoided eye contact too. Bhaskaran got to know the whole story through Krishnan about Anjie's adventure to find her mother.

Anjie was lying down, keeping her head on Aunt Rema's lap outside grandpa's room, narrating her times with her mother, and all others were keenly listening to her. She was explaining how she felt when she saw the laced curtains in her mother's drawing room and the laced dining table cloth. Those laced clothes used to catch her eyes wherever she found them since her childhood, and it was a déjà vu at her mother's cottage. Aunt Rema also agreed that it was indeed a subconscious mind image. Anjie suddenly recalled Aunt Rema studied Psychology for her undergraduate degree in Arts college. Each one was bombarding her with various questions regarding her mother. To help her out from the situation, Aunt Rema pointed to a photograph in the film gossip magazine she was reading and diverted the topic. She explained to Anjie that this man had risen as a new hero of Malayalam (Vernacular language) movies, and his name was Mammootty. She further explained with pride in her eyes that he was her college mate. Aunt Rema said his new movie named Vadakkan Veeragadha (a historic epic drama in vernacular language) based on a medieval ballad from South India, is playing in movie theatres and running house full. Anjie loved to watch Malayalam movies, and they both decided to watch one of his movies together before Anjie leaves for England. Suddenly, all of them got distracted hearing a cry from inside and heard someone's wail. Was it Thangavel uncle's? "AYYYOOOO Achaaa"* (Oh, Father). All of the audience that had surrounded Anjie rushed inside.

Yes, her Grandpa, her beloved Appa, has left this earth. Anjie, while getting up from the verandah, could sense her body shivering with grief. Without her knowledge, tears started pouring. Through the tears, she saw the weaver bird feeding its chicks on the golden shower tree; the decoy nest was not seen anywhere. Anjie's grandfather was placed on the funeral pyre, and his first-born son, Bhaskaran, lit the pyre. Raghavan was wearing the sweater knitted by Anjie's mother, his first son's wife, whom he had not even met once. Anjie got the answer, and she had filled in the blanks for her grandfather too. Anjelina Bhaskaran has a family and an answer to her ethnicity too.

The weaver bird was seen knitting a new nest now on the golden shower tree while Anjie bid tearful goodbye to all in Cochin. Aunt Rema already had a tomato face, and it resembled Anjie on the day she tried to colour her hair black. It was due to her coarsely wiping off the tears from her face. Anjie will board the British Airways flight from Mumbai after alighting from Air India. All her relatives in Cochin stayed for a while at the airport till they could see the Air India flight take off to the skies, and all of them simply stared towards the sky, all with welling eyes.

Bye Bye, Appa

* * *

Name of the Characters

Anjelina (Anjie) – The protagonist

Raghavan – Anjie's Grand father

Bhaskaran – Anjie's father

Malathi – Anjie's Stepmother

Divakaran, Thangavel, Unnikrishnan – Paternal uncles of Anjie

Shyamala, Sarojaya, Premila – Wives of the uncles

Rema – The favourite aunt of Anjelina (her father's younger sister)

Dakshayani – Anjelina's Paternal Grand mother

Margaratte – Estranged mother of Anjelina

James – Anjelina's half brother through her mother's first marriage

Indhulekha, Chandralekha and, Chithralekha – Anjelina's half-sisters through her father's second marriage

About the Illustrator

<u>The illustrations courtesy: Anunanda Unni</u>

<u>About Anunanda Unni</u>

Anunanda Unni is a 25 y/o sprightly soul with equal enthusiasm for life, law, and art. She completed her LL.M. in International Law from IIT Kharagpur, where she would frequently be spotted with a pencil and a sketchbook, the self-taught artist in her growing to find inspiration in everyday working of life. Anu is an enrolled advocate by profession but always an artist at heart!

Connect with Anu at anunandaunni01@gmail.com and follow her creative pursuit on Instagram @talking_tomuch_brushes.

Synopsis

Nestled in the cramped streets of Fort Kochi, where the mosquitos swamped on the leaves and bred in uncountable numbers was Anjie's grandpa's home, a small Mangalore tile roofed house which was home to three generations. As a patriarch of a large family, Raghavan a demur septuagenarian leads a very disciplined life.

All other Men of the family except Raghavan's elder son, literally enjoyed a lethargic parasitic life. The other sons of Raghavan used all possible tactics to continue their idle life by revolving in and out of Fort Kochi, without any proper income. Raghavan orchestrated the entire family show with the assistance of his elder son Bhaskaran, who was in England. Bhaskaran was obliged to provide financial assistance to his father, as his daughter Anjelina, from his British estranged wife was under the guardianship of Raghavan.

The novel is woven around this blue-eyed girl with Anglo features named Anjelina Bhaskaran, wherein she frequently gets confused about her ethnicity due to her anglicized appearance. Anjie was eager to see her younger siblings who lived in England so every 6 months her father will send her photographs of his new family, which was a valuable treasure for her. She used to take it to school and show it to her friends with a pride. They all used to ask her why she was looking quite different from her family, so she eventually stopped showing it to them. But she wanted an answer and set out on a treasure hunt to get one.